Egocentrism and Politics in the Trump Era

Iraya Ahemón García

Published by Doble A, 2024.

While every precaution has been taken in the preparation of this book, the publisher assumes no responsibility for errors or omissions, or for damages resulting from the use of the information contained herein.

EGOCENTRISM AND POLITICS IN THE TRUMP ERA

First edition. October 20, 2024.

Copyright © 2024 Iraya Ahemón García.

ISBN: 979-8227440136

Written by Iraya Ahemón García.

Table of Contents

Egocentrism and Politics in the Trump Era 1
Chapter 1: Origins and Trajectory of Donald Trump 7
Chapter 2: The 2016 Presidential Campaign 15
Chapter 3: Donald Trump's Presidency: First Term (2017-2021) 23
Chapter 4: Foreign Policy and International Relations..................31
Chapter 5: The Second Campaign and the 2020 Election 41
Chapter 6: The Unachieved Second Term and the End of the Presidency..49
Chapter 7: Donald Trump's Legacy..59
Chapter 8: Donald Trump's Style and Personality 69
Chapter 9: Criticisms and Controversies 77
Chapter 10: The Capitol Attack (January 6, 2021) 85
Chapter 11: The Assassination Attempt on Donald Trump and Its Repercussions on the 2024 Campaign 89
Chapter 12: Future Prospects and Lasting Legacy 91
Epilogue: The Future of American Politics 99
Sources consulted 103

Introduction

In the political history of the United States, few names resonate as strongly as Donald Trump's. His rise to the presidency in 2016 marked a turning point in American politics, sparking a wave of debates, passions, and controversies that shook the foundations of the country and captured the world's attention. However, beyond the newspaper headlines and breaking news stories, there is a deeper narrative that deserves exploration.

This book delves into the life and presidency of Donald Trump, from his beginnings in the heart of New York to his controversial tenure in the White House. Throughout the following pages, we will uncover the details of his personal life, his career in the business world, and his surprising foray into politics, painting a complete and nuanced portrait of a figure who polarized the nation like few before him.

As we explore Donald Trump's legacy, we do not seek to pass definitive judgments or take sides. Instead, our goal is to provide readers with an impartial and balanced view of the events, policies, and personalities that shaped his presidency. We will do so through a thorough exploration of the chapters that make up this book, each of which focuses on key aspects of his life and his time in office.

From his family roots and education to his rise to the presidency and his impact on global politics, these pages explore the many facets of Donald Trump as a leader, businessman, communicator, and above all, as an influential historical figure. Throughout this journey, readers will discover how his bold style and political decisions provoked passionate reactions from both sides of the political spectrum, and how his presidency left an indelible mark on the contemporary history of the United States.

Whether admired or criticized, it is undeniable that the Trump phenomenon has left a profound impression on the American political landscape. This book aims to shed light on the man behind the rhetoric and offer readers a deeper understanding of one of the most extraordinary moments in U.S. political history. Without further ado, we invite you to explore the life and legacy of Donald J. Trump.

Political and social context before Trump's presidency

To provide political and social context before Donald Trump's presidency, it is important to address several key aspects that defined the situation in the United States in the years leading up to his election in 2016:

1. Previous presidencies: Before Donald Trump, the United States had two consecutive Democratic presidents: Bill Clinton (1993-2001) and Barack Obama (2009-2017). Each faced significant challenges during their terms, including the 2008 economic recession and struggles over healthcare reform (Obamacare).
2. Economic crisis and recovery: The 2008 financial crisis left lasting economic effects in the U.S. and around the world. While the U.S. economy had begun to recover, many Americans still felt the recession's impact, including job losses and declining wealth.
3. Party politics: U.S. politics were characterized by increasing partisan polarization. Congress was divided, with Republicans controlling the House of Representatives and Democrats controlling the Senate for much of Obama's presidency. This polarization made it difficult to pass important legislation and led to frustration among voters.
4. Immigration and border security: Immigration was a hot-button issue before Trump's presidency. Debates raged over border security, illegal immigration, and the status of the Dreamers (young undocumented immigrants who arrived in the U.S. as children).
5. Demographic changes: The U.S. was undergoing significant demographic shifts. The Latino population and other

minority groups were growing rapidly, with political and cultural implications.
6. Global challenges: U.S. foreign policy was marked by international challenges such as the war in Afghanistan, the fight against ISIS in Iraq and Syria, tensions with Russia and China, and international agreements on climate change.
7. Media and social networks: The proliferation of social media and the transformation of the media industry played a significant role in U.S. politics. Social media became a key platform for political communication and information dissemination.
8. Social movements: Several major social movements emerged during this period, such as the Occupy Wall Street movement and Black Lives Matter, highlighting issues of economic and racial inequality.
9. Distrust in institutions: There was growing distrust in political and governmental institutions, as well as traditional media. This contributed to the appeal of candidates who positioned themselves as "outsiders" to the established system.

This political and social context provides the backdrop for a better understanding of Donald Trump's presidency and how his policies and approaches responded to the challenges and concerns of the time.

Donald Trump's public image before the presidency

Donald Trump's public image before his presidency is crucial to understanding his political rise and popularity at the time. Here is an overview of how Donald Trump presented himself in the public sphere before his election as president:

1. Real estate mogul: Donald Trump was widely known as a successful real estate magnate. His family had a background in real estate, and he made a name for himself in New York and beyond with his real estate development projects, including

the construction of Trump Tower in Manhattan and the Trump International Hotel and Tower in Chicago.
2. Businessman and personal brand: Trump presented himself as a successful businessman and a symbol of business success. He often used the catchphrase "You're Fired" on his reality show "The Apprentice," where he played the role of host and judge. This television exposure boosted his public profile and personal brand.
3. Author and writer: Trump wrote several books, including "The Art of the Deal," which became a bestseller. These books reflected his views on business and success.
4. Charismatic and controversial personality: Trump was known for his charismatic personality and his direct, sometimes controversial style. He often spoke frankly and unfiltered in interviews and public speeches, which garnered both admiration and criticism.
5. Political involvement and controversies: Before his presidency, Trump had occasionally flirted with politics. In 2000, he briefly ran as a candidate for the Reform Party. He was also an outspoken critic of the Barack Obama administration and had promoted conspiracy theories about Obama's birthplace.
6. Political contributions: Trump made financial contributions to various political candidates and parties, both Democratic and Republican, over the years. This connected him to politics, although he was not a career politician at the time.
7. Involvement in controversial issues: Trump participated in public debates on issues such as climate change and immigration policy, often expressing polarizing opinions that drew media attention.
8. Social media presence: Trump actively used social media, especially Twitter, to communicate with the public, express

his opinions, and criticize his opponents. His tweets often made headlines and had a significant impact on the public conversation.

This portrayal of Donald Trump as a public figure before his presidency established him as a recognized and controversial figure in American life, which later helped him in his political career and eventual election as the 45th president of the United States. His direct style and ability to connect with a segment of the electorate were key elements in his political rise.

Chapter 1: Origins and Trajectory of Donald Trump

Before the world knew him as president, before his name echoed through the corridors of the White House and in news headlines around the globe, Donald John Trump was a child born in Queens, New York, with dreams and ambitions like any other. In this first chapter, we delve into the foundations of the figure who would become the 45th president of the United States, a figure whose origins and personal trajectory forged a path that would leave an indelible mark on history.

Born on June 14, 1946, Donald Trump came into the world at a time of profound changes in the United States and the world. His childhood and adolescence within an immigrant family of German and Scottish-Irish descent laid the groundwork for his character and his perspective on life. Through accounts from relatives, friends, and people close to him in his early years, we explore the values and influences that shaped him.

But Donald Trump did not limit himself to following a conventional path. From his days as a student at a military academy to his entry into the Wharton School of Business at the University of Pennsylvania, his educational choices and his first steps in the business world charted a course that would lead him to the top of the business world and, ultimately, to politics.

During his career in real estate, Trump became a prominent figure in New York and beyond. From the construction of iconic skyscrapers to his forays into the world of entertainment and television, his name became synonymous with success and unbridled ambition.

As we progress through this chapter, we will explore the challenges and triumphs that marked his path to fame and national recognition. We will meet the key people who influenced his life and the decisions that led him to the pinnacle of business and, finally, to the center stage of American politics.

Family Background and Education
Trump Family: Roots and Influences

The origins of Donald John Trump trace back to an immigrant family. His paternal grandfather, Friedrich Trump, arrived in the United States from Germany in the late 19th century, seeking opportunities in the land of possibilities. His entrepreneurial vision would be reflected in future generations of the Trump family.

Donald's father, Frederick Christ Trump, was a prominent real estate entrepreneur in Queens, New York. Through his company, Elizabeth Trump & Son, he dedicated himself to building single-family homes and apartments, establishing a solid economic foundation for the family.

Donald Trump, the fourth of five children, was born on June 14, 1946, at Jamaica Hospital Medical Center, Queens. He grew up in a brick house in the neighborhood of Jamaica Estates, where his family resided in a prosperous, upper-middle-class area.

Education and Early Formation

Donald Trump's early education took place at the Kew-Forest School in Queens, a private school for children. His rebellious behavior and uncontainable energy led his parents to enroll him in the New York Military Academy (NYMA) at the age of 13. NYMA emphasized discipline and leadership, and Donald excelled in sports, especially baseball and football.

After graduating from NYMA, Trump continued his education at Fordham University in the Bronx, before transferring to the prestigious

EGOCENTRISM AND POLITICS IN THE TRUMP ERA

Wharton School of Business at the University of Pennsylvania in 1966. At Wharton, Trump earned a Bachelor's degree in Economics in 1968. Throughout his education, Trump displayed his ambition and incipient entrepreneurial skills.

These early years and the influence of his family and educators provided the foundations for what would become a career in the business world and, eventually, in politics. Donald Trump emerged from his education and family environment with an entrepreneurial spirit, iron determination, and a relentless desire for success. These qualities, combined with his education and family background, would form the platform from which he would build his business empire and, ultimately, his political trajectory.

First Steps in the Business World

After graduating from the University of Pennsylvania in 1968, Donald Trump returned to New York and joined his father's real estate company, Elizabeth Trump & Son. His father, Fred Trump, had established a solid real estate empire centered in Queens and Brooklyn, building single-family homes and apartments.

Donald Trump learned the fundamentals of the real estate business from his father, from property acquisition to managing construction projects. However, his ambitions would take him beyond the neighborhoods of Queens.

Trump Tower and the Leap to Manhattan

In 1971, Donald Trump moved to Manhattan and began to get involved in more ambitious real estate projects. In 1974, he acquired the Commodore Hotel building on 42nd Street, which would later be transformed into the Grand Hyatt Hotel. This project marked his entry into the Manhattan real estate world and was a precursor of what was to come.

In 1978, Trump began working on what would become one of his most iconic projects: the construction of Trump Tower on Fifth

Avenue. This 68-story skyscraper, with its characteristic glass and brass facade, would become a symbol of luxury and opulence in New York.

Trump Tower, completed in 1983, marked the beginning of a series of real estate developments in Manhattan that would bear the Trump name. Trump Plaza, Trump Palace, and other high-rise buildings were erected in the city, consolidating his reputation as a renowned real estate developer.

Business Outside New York

As his success in Manhattan grew, Donald Trump expanded his reach beyond New York. He ventured into the world of casinos and hotels in Atlantic City, New Jersey, and acquired properties in other parts of the United States. In addition to real estate, Trump diversified his investments in fields such as aviation, sports, and entertainment.

The Trump Empire

In the 1980s and 1990s, Donald Trump had built a business empire that encompassed real estate, casinos, golf courses, and more. His personal brand became synonymous with luxury and success.

This stage of his business life was not without challenges. Trump experienced financial ups and downs and was involved in litigation. However, his ability to recover from adversity and maintain his public profile allowed him to stay at the top of the business world.

Donald Trump's career in business and the real estate world was a mix of bold ambition, iconic projects, and moments of crisis. His ability to navigate this tumultuous business landscape would be a significant factor in his subsequent foray into politics and his election as President of the United States.

Participation in Television Programs
The Rise to Fame on the Small Screen

As Donald Trump continued to expand his empire in real estate and business, he also embarked on a new adventure in the world of television entertainment. In 2004, he made his small screen debut as the host of an innovative reality TV show titled "The Apprentice."

EGOCENTRISM AND POLITICS IN THE TRUMP ERA

The concept of the show was simple but intriguing: aspiring entrepreneurs competed in business challenges, and the winner had the opportunity to work in one of Trump's companies with a six-figure salary. Donald Trump, with his characteristic direct style and his phrase "You're Fired," became the face and driving force of this exciting program.

Impact on Pop Culture

"The Apprentice" quickly became a ratings hit and captured the attention of audiences across the country. Viewers were intrigued by the dynamics between the competitors, the challenging business tests, and, of course, Trump's charismatic presence as the main judge.

The phrase "You're Fired" became a popular slogan, and the image of Trump in his luxury office in Trump Tower became iconic. The show was not only a success in terms of viewership, but it also further solidified the Trump brand and his image as a successful businessman and authority figure.

The Trump Brand and Politics

Trump's participation in "The Apprentice" helped consolidate his status as an influential public figure, which would ultimately impact his political career. As his public profile grew, he began to express political opinions and participated in public debates on hot-button issues, such as President Barack Obama's birthplace.

The constant exposure on television and his presence in pop culture paved the way for his foray into politics and his eventual candidacy for the presidency in 2016. His television experience provided him with the ability to communicate effectively with the public and leverage his fame to build a base of loyal followers.

In summary, Donald Trump's participation in television programs, particularly in "'The Apprentice," was an essential component of his rise to prominence in American popular culture and politics. This media exposure played a significant role in his eventual election as President of the United States.

IRAYA AHEMÓN GARCÍA

Personality and Psychological Profile of Donald Trump

The analysis of Donald Trump's personality and psychological profile is a complex topic subject to various interpretations. Throughout his public life and presidency, Trump exhibited a series of personality traits and behaviors that generated widespread debate and analysis by psychologists and mental health experts. Below are some of the characteristics and personality traits that have often been discussed in relation to Donald Trump:

1. Narcissism: One of the terms that has been associated with Trump is narcissism. His elevated self-esteem, his need for constant attention, and his belief in his personal superiority are traits that some experts have linked to narcissism.
2. Constant self-affirmation: Trump is known for his tendency to constantly praise his own abilities and achievements, and often resorts to self-affirmation in speeches and social media.
3. Direct and unfiltered communication: Trump is famous for his direct and unfiltered communication style, in which he often uses strong and colloquial language. Some see it as a display of authenticity, while others criticize it for its lack of decorum.
4. Polarization: During his presidency, Trump was a highly polarizing figure. His rhetoric and focus on divisive issues often generated strong reactions of both support and opposition.
5. Impulsivity: Trump sometimes made impulsive and quick decisions, which generated controversy and surprise both nationally and internationally.
6. Resistance to criticism: Trump often showed stubborn resistance to criticism and a tendency to attack those who questioned him, whether in the media or in politics.
7. Political acumen: Despite his controversial style, Trump

demonstrated political skills in mobilizing a loyal base of supporters and using effective strategies in elections.

It is important to note that the analysis of the personality and psychological profile of a public figure like Trump is complex and controversial. These characteristics and traits are only general observations based on his public behavior. The diagnosis of a specific mental health condition can only be made by mental health professionals in a clinical setting and with access to detailed information.

The Influence of the Psychological Profile on the Implementation of His Policies

The possible influence of Donald Trump's psychological profile on the implementation of his policies is a topic of constant debate and analysis. Although it is important to remember that a definitive psychological diagnosis of a person cannot be made without proper clinical evaluation, patterns of behavior and personality traits can be identified that could have influenced his political decisions and leadership style. Below, some of the possible influences are explored:

1. Impulsive decision-making: If Trump has impulsive tendencies, this could have influenced the speed with which he made political decisions, especially in crisis situations. His decision-making style was often characterized by immediate actions and public statements without a prolonged deliberation process.
2. Tendency towards polarization: His polarizing personality could have contributed to his focus on policies and speeches that generated divisions in society. The policies he promoted, such as immigration and healthcare, often generated highly polarized debates.
3. Resistance to criticism: Resistance to criticism and the tendency to attack opponents or critics could have influenced

his approach to political communication. Trump often responded to criticism with counterattacks rather than seeking compromise or collaboration.
4. Prioritization of personal message: His need for constant attention and self-affirmation could have influenced his approach to promoting his own image and achievements, sometimes at the expense of balanced attention to political and public policy issues.
5. Direct communication: His direct and unfiltered communication style could have influenced the way he communicated with the public and his ability to connect with a part of the population that valued his frankness.

The influence of Trump's psychological profile on his policies is a complex topic subject to interpretation. Historians and political analysts continue to debate this issue and how his personality may have influenced his approach to governing and decision-making.

Chapter 2: The 2016 Presidential Campaign

The year 2016 will be remembered as a turning point in the political history of the United States. It was a year in which conventional political expectations crumbled and a singular candidate, Donald J. Trump, ascended to the political stage with a campaign that defied all odds. In this second chapter, we delve into the exciting and often unpredictable journey that marked the 2016 presidential campaign.

The country was divided, tensions were palpable, and American politics had never before witnessed such an intense and polarized electoral contest. At the epicenter of this whirlwind was Donald Trump, a businessman and television celebrity who had transformed into an unprecedented political phenomenon.

This chapter immerses us in the origins of Trump's campaign, from the first rumors about his possible candidacy to the official launch of his campaign in June 2015. We will explore the central themes that drove his platform, from immigration to the economy and international trade, and how his approach resonated with a loyal base of followers.

The 2016 presidential campaign was also characterized by its brutality and confrontation. Debates, personal attacks, and last-minute surprises set the tone, and Donald Trump, with his unfiltered style and ability to dominate news headlines, became the center of attention.

We will meet the key players in this campaign, from political advisors to opponents within and outside his own party. We will examine the crucial moments, from the primaries to the conventions, and how Trump finally secured the Republican nomination.

This chapter is a journey through a presidential campaign that defied expectations and forever changed the political landscape of the United States. As we explore the events, strategies, and tactics that led to Trump's surprising victory in November 2016, we also discover how American politics would enter a new era under his leadership.

Announcement of Candidacy

The announcement of Donald Trump's candidacy for the presidency in 2016 was a historic and key moment in his political rise.

On June 16, 2015, in the iconic Trump Tower in New York, with a golden stage and twinkling lights prepared for the event, Donald J. Trump took a bold step that would change the course of American politics. Surrounded by a crowd of eager supporters and journalists, Trump approached the podium with a confident and determined expression on his face.

"Today, I announce my candidacy for the presidency of the United States. I'm here to tell you that our country is in ruins. Our economy is in ruins. Our military is in ruins. Our immigration system is in ruins. Our foreign policy is in ruins. And, worst of all, our confidence in ourselves is in ruins."

The atmosphere was charged with expectation as the businessman and television personality prepared to make the announcement that would shock the world. Flanked by a large banner proclaiming "Make America Great Again," Trump began his speech.

In his characteristic style, Trump referred to himself as a "successful businessman" and spoke about his concern for the state of the nation. He described problems such as illegal immigration, job loss, and lack of leadership in Washington as reasons for his candidacy.

In his speech, Trump promised to "regain control" of the United States and emphasized his focus on the economy and job creation. He also launched sharp criticisms at the established political class, claiming they were responsible for the country's problems.

Trump's announcement was shocking and polarizing from the start. His frank rhetoric and unfiltered style resonated with some voters seeking radical change in politics, while generating controversy and fiercely partisan criticism.

Among those announcements were the following that would mark his policy once he won the election:

"I promise to build a wall on the border between the United States and Mexico. I promise to deport all illegal immigrants. I promise to renegotiate our country's trade agreements. I promise to make our military strong again. I promise to make our economy great again. I promise to make our country safe again. And I promise to make our country great again."

The announcement of his candidacy marked the beginning of an extraordinary presidential campaign that defied all expectations and led Donald Trump, an outsider in the world of politics, to secure the Republican nomination and ultimately become the 45th president of the United States. His direct style and promise to "make America great again" resonated deeply with a significant portion of the American electorate and forever changed the country's political landscape.

Campaign Strategies

Donald Trump's 2016 presidential campaign was one of the most controversial and successful campaigns in U.S. history. Trump, a multi-millionaire businessman and former reality TV star, presented himself as an outsider who promised to "make America great again."

One of the key strategies of Trump's campaign was the use of social media. Trump was a master at using Twitter to spread his message and connect with his followers. His messages, often inflammatory and controversial, generated significant media attention and helped keep his name in the headlines.

Another key strategy of Trump's campaign was focusing on discontented voters. Trump appealed to voters who felt the political system was broken and their needs were not being met. His promises to build a wall on the border with Mexico, deport illegal immigrants, and renegotiate the country's trade agreements resonated with these voters.

Trump also used a "scorched earth" strategy against his Democratic opponent, Hillary Clinton. His personal attacks against Clinton were fierce and merciless. This helped polarize the electorate and mobilize his supporters.

Ultimately, Trump's strategy was successful. He won the presidential election, defeating Clinton by a difference of 77 electoral votes.

Here's a summary of some of the key strategies he employed during his campaign:

1. Direct and controversial messages: Trump adopted a direct and unfiltered communication style that allowed him to stand out in a field of Republican candidates. His speeches and statements were often controversial and sometimes inflammatory, ensuring constant media coverage.

2. Focus on discontented voters: Trump appealed to voters who felt the political system was broken and their needs were not being met. His promises to build a wall on the border with Mexico, deport illegal immigrants, and renegotiate the country's trade agreements resonated with these voters.

3. Focus on populist issues: Trump focused on populist issues such as immigration, international trade, and job loss in the United States. He promised to "Make America Great Again" and fought against what he called "the Washington establishment," connecting with voters who felt marginalized by traditional politics.

4. Effective use of social media: Trump was a pioneer in using social media as a campaign tool. His active presence on Twitter allowed him

to communicate directly with his base of followers and dominate the news 24 hours a day.

5. Challenge to political correctness: Trump openly challenged political correctness, a strategy that resonated with many voters who were tired of what they perceived as politically correct speech. This allowed him to stand out as an "outsider" in politics.

6. Mass rallies and visual communication: He organized massive campaign events across the country, attracting thousands of followers. His campaign logo and the slogan "Make America Great Again" became iconic visual elements.

7. Personal attacks on opponents: During the primaries and general campaign, Trump did not hesitate to launch personal attacks on his opponents, both inside and outside his party. These attacks often generated headlines and kept attention on his candidacy.

8. Tour of crucial states: Trump focused on key states that would later give him victory in the Electoral College, such as Pennsylvania, Wisconsin, and Michigan. His strategy focused on winning in these states instead of focusing on the popular vote.

9. Mobilization of the base: Trump mobilized a base of loyal and enthusiastic supporters who actively participated in the campaign and voted in record numbers.

10. Participation in Presidential Debates: Despite being his first foray into politics, Trump participated effectively in the presidential debates, defending his views and maintaining the support of his base.

These strategies, along with a series of unforeseen factors, contributed to Donald Trump's surprising victory in the 2016 presidential election. His campaign was an example of how an unconventional candidate can use unusual tactics to win his party's nomination and then the presidency.

Key Themes and Campaign Promises

Donald Trump's 2016 presidential campaign focused on several key themes and promises that resonated with his base of supporters and helped define his platform. Below are some of the most prominent themes and key promises of his campaign:

1. Immigration: One of the most prominent themes of Trump's campaign was immigration. He promised to take tougher measures against illegal immigration, build a wall on the border with Mexico, and reform the immigration system to prioritize U.S. interests and security.

2. Economy and jobs: Trump presented himself as a successful businessman and promised to revitalize the American economy. He advocated for tax cuts, elimination of business regulations, and renegotiation of international trade agreements, such as the North American Free Trade Agreement (NAFTA).

3. Healthcare: Trump promised to repeal and replace the Affordable Care Act (Obamacare), which had been a flagship policy of the Barack Obama administration. He sought a reform of the healthcare system that would offer more options and reduce costs.

4. National security and fight against terrorism: Trump emphasized the importance of strengthening national security and taking tougher measures against terrorism. He advocated for greater surveillance of Muslim immigrants and a more aggressive strategy against terrorist groups abroad.

5. Foreign policy and trade: Trump adopted a more unilateral approach to foreign policy and promised to renegotiate international trade agreements, such as the Trans-Pacific Partnership (TPP) and the Paris Climate Agreement. He also expressed skepticism about traditional U.S. alliances, such as NATO.

6. Fight against crime and violence: Trump committed to being "the law and order president" and promised to address the increase in violence in some U.S. cities. He advocated for greater law enforcement and a tougher stance on crime.

7. Foreign trade policy: Trump advocated for a more protectionist approach to foreign trade policy, with an emphasis on creating jobs in the United States and renegotiating unfavorable trade agreements.

Some of Trump's specific campaign promises included:

- Build a wall on the border between the United States and Mexico, and have Mexico pay for it.
- Deport all illegal immigrants, except children.
- Renegotiate NAFTA to make it more favorable for the United States.
- Reduce taxes for businesses and high-income individuals.
- Cut government regulation.
- Strengthen the U.S. military.
- Combat terrorism.
- Curb illegal immigration.
- Put America first in its international relations.
- Renegotiate trade treaties with other countries.
- Withdraw from the Paris Agreement on climate change.

These are just some of the key themes and promises of Trump's 2016 campaign. His focus on these issues, along with his direct and unfiltered communication style, resonated with a significant portion of the American electorate and led him to victory in the Electoral College in November 2016, despite losing the popular vote to his opponent, Hillary Clinton.

Chapter 3: Donald Trump's Presidency: First Term (2017-2021)

On a cold winter morning in Washington D.C., on January 20, 2017, Donald John Trump took the oath of office as the 45th president of the United States. This historic event marked the beginning of a political chapter that captivated the world's attention. Trump's first term was characterized by a series of challenges, controversies, and significant changes that left a deep mark on U.S. history.

This third chapter of our journey will immerse you in the complex and fascinating dynamics of Trump's presidency during his first term. Throughout these four years, the White House witnessed a series of policies and decisions that resonated throughout the country and beyond its borders. From immigration policy changes and tax reforms to clashes with world leaders and managing unexpected crises, Trump's presidency was a period of turbulence and transformation.

We will explore his focus on the economy and how he sought to revitalize it through tax cuts and deregulation. We will examine his efforts to reform the healthcare system, including his battle against the Affordable Care Act (Obamacare). We will also analyze his trade policies, his stance on national security, and his approach to fighting terrorism.

However, we cannot overlook the controversies and challenges that marked his presidency, including the investigation into Russian interference in the elections, international relationship tensions, and the government's response to the COVID-19 pandemic.

As we progress through this chapter, we will explore how Trump's policies and personality continued to divide the nation, sparking passionate debates and partisan confrontations. We will also see how his actions and decisions influenced domestic politics and the U.S.'s position on the global stage.

Donald Trump's presidency during his first term left an indelible mark on U.S. political history and defined an era of polarized politics and fervent debates. As we examine these crucial years, we will delve into the heart of a presidential administration that left a lasting legacy and will continue to be the subject of discussion and analysis for decades to come.

Inauguration and Early Days in Office

The inauguration and early days of Donald Trump's presidency in January 2017 were historic moments filled with high expectations. Here's a description of those key moments:

Presidential Inauguration (January 20, 2017)

On January 20, 2017, under a winter sky in Washington D.C., Donald Trump's presidential inauguration took place. Millions of people gathered in the city to witness this event, while millions more watched from across the country and the world through media broadcasts.

In his inaugural address, Trump delivered his famous phrase "America First," reiterating his commitment to prioritize American interests in all his policies. He also spoke of a "bleeding" America and promised to tackle what he saw as urgent problems, such as illegal immigration, job losses, and the threat of terrorism.

The inauguration marked the starting point for his presidency, and his speech made it clear that his approach would be disruptive and different from his predecessors.

Early Days in Office

After taking office, Donald Trump quickly began implementing his agenda. Some of the notable early actions of his presidency included:

EGOCENTRISM AND POLITICS IN THE TRUMP ERA

1. Executive Orders: Trump issued a series of executive orders in his first days in office. This included actions related to repealing parts of the Affordable Care Act (Obamacare), building the border wall with Mexico, and withdrawing the U.S. from the Trans-Pacific Partnership (TPP).
2. Cabinet Appointments: Trump appointed several members to his cabinet, including Secretary of State Rex Tillerson, Secretary of Defense James Mattis, and Secretary of the Treasury Steven Mnuchin.
3. Tax Reform: In December 2017, Congress passed a significant tax reform, which included tax cuts for both individuals and businesses. This was one of the key promises of his campaign and one of the early legislative achievements of his presidency.
4. Immigration Policy: Trump signed a series of executive orders related to immigration, including a travel ban on certain majority-Muslim countries and the repeal of the Deferred Action for Childhood Arrivals (DACA) program.
5. Supreme Court Nomination: In January 2017, Trump nominated Judge Neil Gorsuch to fill a vacant seat on the U.S. Supreme Court, a decision that had a lasting impact on the court's composition.

Here are some key events from Trump's inauguration and early days in office:

- January 20, 2017: Donald Trump is sworn in as the 45th president of the United States.
- January 20, 2017: Trump signs an executive order to build a wall along the U.S.-Mexico border.
- January 20, 2017: Trump signs an executive order banning travel to the U.S. from seven majority-Muslim countries.
- January 21, 2017: Trump signs an executive order to withdraw the U.S. from the Paris Agreement on climate change.

- January 27, 2017: Trump meets with Mexican President Enrique Peña Nieto to discuss the border wall.
- January 28, 2017: Trump signs an executive order to repeal the Affordable Care Act, also known as Obamacare.

These early days and actions set the tone for Donald Trump's presidency and reflected his political priorities and approach to key issues. The Trump administration was characterized by its disruptive style and willingness to take bold measures to fulfill campaign promises.

Key Policies and Achievements

During his first term (2017-2021), Donald Trump's presidency was marked by a series of significant policies and achievements that influenced the country's direction and sparked intense political debate. Here's an overview of some of the most notable policies and accomplishments:

1. **Tax Reform**: One of the most prominent achievements of the Trump administration was the passage of a tax reform in December 2017. This reform reduced tax rates for individuals and corporations, easing the tax burden for many people and businesses. The law also included the elimination of the individual mandate penalty from Obamacare.
2. **Supreme Court Nominations**: Trump nominated three justices to the U.S. Supreme Court during his term: Neil Gorsuch in 2017, Brett Kavanaugh in 2018, and Amy Coney Barrett in 2020. These nominations shifted the court's composition towards a conservative majority, which had a lasting impact on the court's political balance.
3. **Deregulation**: The Trump administration focused on deregulation, arguing that it would spur economic growth and reduce bureaucracy. Significant regulatory reductions were implemented in areas such as energy, the environment,

and financial services.
4. **Immigration Policy**: The Trump administration implemented stricter immigration policies, including the construction of additional sections of border wall, the repeal of DACA (Deferred Action for Childhood Arrivals), and restrictions on legal immigration.
5. **Trade Negotiations:** Trump engaged in tough trade negotiations, including the renegotiation of the North American Free Trade Agreement (NAFTA), which became the U.S.-Mexico-Canada Agreement (USMCA). He also embarked on a trade war with China, imposing tariffs on Chinese imports.
6. **Criminal Justice Reform:** In December 2018, Trump signed the First Step Act, a bipartisan criminal justice reform law aimed at addressing issues in the justice system and reducing mandatory minimum sentences for certain non-violent offenses.
7. **ISIS Fight:** The Trump administration intensified military efforts against the Islamic State (ISIS) in the Middle East, achieving the group's territorial defeat in Syria and Iraq.
8. **COVID-19 Vaccine Development:** Although the COVID-19 pandemic significantly impacted his presidency, the Trump administration played a role in Operation Warp Speed, which accelerated the development and distribution of COVID-19 vaccines.

Some of Trump's specific achievements include:

- The unemployment rate reached a historic low of 3.5% in 2019.
- Average economic growth during Trump's term was 2.3%.
- The U.S. signed new trade agreements with Mexico, Canada, and Japan.

- Trump achieved partial denuclearization of North Korea.

Controversies and Challenges

Donald Trump's presidency during his first term was marked by a series of controversies and challenges that generated intense debate and tensions both in the country and the international community. Below are some of the major controversies and challenges of his term:

1. **Russian Election Interference Investigation:** One of the most prominent controversies was the investigation into Russian interference in the 2016 election and possible connections between Trump's campaign and Russia. The appointment of Special Counsel Robert Mueller to investigate these matters kept the country's attention for several years, although no evidence of criminal conspiracy between Trump's campaign and Russia was found.
2. **International Relations:** Trump often took a unilateral approach to international relations, creating tensions with traditional allies. His trade policies, tariffs, and withdrawals from international agreements like the Paris Climate Agreement and the Iran nuclear deal were sources of controversy.
3. **Immigration Policy:** Trump's immigration policy was a constant source of controversy. His family separation policies at the border, the cancellation of DACA, and restrictions on legal immigration led to widespread criticism and protests.
4. **COVID-19 Pandemic Management:** The Trump administration's response to the COVID-19 pandemic was a subject of debate and controversy. Criticisms included a lack of national coordination, disputes over mask usage, and challenges in securing and distributing medical supplies.
5. **Communication and Social Media:** Trump's direct and unfiltered communication style, especially on Twitter, often

generated controversy and criticism. His tweets and public statements could be divisive and provoke passionate reactions.

6. **Impeachment Process:** Trump faced two impeachment processes in the House of Representatives, in 2019 and 2021. The first process centered on allegations of abuse of power and obstruction of Congress related to Ukraine, while the second was based on his role in the events of January 6, 2021, at the U.S. Capitol.
7. **Protests and Racial Tensions:** During his term, there were significant protests and tensions related to racial and social issues. Events like the death of George Floyd and the subsequent unrest sparked a national debate on racial justice and law enforcement.
8. **Scandals and Allegations:** Trump was accused of sexual harassment by several women and was investigated for possible obstruction of justice and false testimony in the investigation into Russian interference in the 2016 presidential election. These accusations damaged his credibility and earned widespread criticism.

Chapter 4: Foreign Policy and International Relations

Foreign policy and international relations immerse us in the complex and multifaceted world of Donald Trump's presidency's foreign policy. During his tenure, the focus on international relations and diplomacy played a crucial role in decision-making and the influence of the United States on the world stage.

Donald Trump's foreign policy and international relations were characterized by a unilateralist and nationalist approach. Trump distanced himself from traditional U.S. alliances and adopted a tougher stance in his relations with other countries.

One of Trump's most controversial policies was the withdrawal of the United States from the Paris Agreement on climate change. Trump argued that the agreement was unfair to the United States and that it would not achieve its objectives. The U.S. withdrawal from the agreement was condemned by most countries in the world.

Trump also withdrew from the North American Free Trade Agreement (NAFTA), a trade agreement between the United States, Canada, and Mexico. Trump argued that NAFTA was a bad deal for the United States and did not benefit American workers. The U.S. withdrawal from NAFTA led to negotiations for a new trade agreement, called the United States-Mexico-Canada Agreement (USMCA).

Trump also imposed tariffs on products from China and other countries. Trump argued that the tariffs were necessary to protect

American jobs and American industry. However, the tariffs sparked a trade war with China that damaged the global economy.

In this chapter, we will explore how the Trump administration addressed crucial issues in the international arena, from trade and traditional alliances to the fight against terrorism and diplomacy with adversary nations. We will examine the challenges and controversies that arose in the international arena and how Trump's presidency impacted U.S. relations with other countries and international organizations.

We will also see how Trump's "America First" approach translated into specific policies and actions in the international arena, including withdrawal from international agreements and treaties, emphasis on national sovereignty, and tough trade negotiations.

As we progress through this chapter, we will have the opportunity to explore how Donald Trump's presidency reshaped the role of the United States on the world stage and how these policies and actions left a lasting mark on the nation's foreign policy and international relations.

Relations with World Leaders

Donald Trump's relationships with world leaders were often tense and conflictive. Trump distanced himself from traditional U.S. alliances and adopted a tougher stance in his relations with other countries.

One of Trump's most difficult relationships was with Mexican President Enrique Peña Nieto. Trump harshly criticized Mexico for illegal immigration and crime, and threatened to impose tariffs on Mexican products. Relations between Trump and Peña Nieto reached a low point in 2017 when Trump canceled a scheduled visit to Mexico.

Trump also had a difficult relationship with Chinese President Xi Jinping. Trump imposed tariffs on Chinese products and criticized China for its trade policy and labor practices. Relations between Trump and Xi Jinping improved in 2019 when both leaders signed a partial trade agreement.

EGOCENTRISM AND POLITICS IN THE TRUMP ERA

Here is a summary of some of the most prominent relationships with world leaders:

1. **Vladimir Putin** (Russia): The relationship between Trump and Russian President Vladimir Putin was the subject of intense attention. Trump expressed on several occasions his desire to improve relations with Russia and met with Putin on several occasions during his tenure. However, these meetings generated controversy due to Russian interference in the 2016 elections and other concerns.
2. **Xi Jinping** (China): Trump maintained a complicated relationship with Chinese President Xi Jinping. He initiated a trade war with China, imposing tariffs on Chinese imports and accusing the country of unfair trade practices. Despite this, they also sought cooperation in areas such as the denuclearization of North Korea.
3. **Kim Jong-un** (North Korea): The relationship with North Korean leader Kim Jong-un was one of the most prominent in Trump's diplomacy. After an escalation of tensions and hostile rhetoric, Trump met twice with Kim in historic summits to discuss North Korea's denuclearization, although these talks did not lead to a definitive agreement.
4. **Angela Merkel** (Germany): The relationship between Trump and German Chancellor Angela Merkel was often tense. They had differences on issues such as trade, climate change, and NATO. Relations between the United States and the European Union also faced challenges during his tenure.
5. **Emmanuel Macron** (France): French President Emmanuel Macron sought to maintain a pragmatic relationship with Trump, although they had differences on issues such as the Paris Agreement and policy towards Iran. Macron also organized international summits with Trump on topics such

as climate change.
6. **Justin Trudeau** (Canada): The relationship with Canadian Prime Minister Justin Trudeau became tense due to trade disputes, particularly over the United States-Mexico-Canada Agreement (USMCA) and steel and aluminum tariffs.
7. Boris Johnson (United Kingdom): Trump expressed support for then-British Prime Minister Boris Johnson during the Brexit process, and both leaders sought to strengthen the special relationship between the United States and the United Kingdom.

These are just some of the key relationships that defined the foreign policy of the Trump administration. Relationships with world leaders varied widely depending on the interests and priorities of each country, and contributed to the complex diplomatic landscape of Trump's presidency.

International Treaties and Agreements

During his presidency, Donald Trump adopted a critical approach to various international treaties and agreements, seeking to renegotiate or withdraw from several of them. Below are some of the most notable treaties and international agreements that were the subject of attention during his tenure:

1. **Paris Climate Agreement**: In June 2017, Donald Trump announced the United States' intention to withdraw from the Paris Agreement on climate change. He argued that the agreement was unfavorable to the U.S. economy and would impose unfair economic costs. The U.S. withdrawal became effective in November 2020, but the Biden administration announced its intention to rejoin the agreement.
2. **Iran Nuclear Deal** (JCPOA): Trump withdrew from the JCPOA (Joint Comprehensive Plan of Action) in May 2018,

arguing that the agreement did not adequately address concerns about Iran's nuclear program. This action led to the reimposition of economic sanctions against Iran and an increase in tensions in the region.
3. **INF Treaty:** In 2019, the United States withdrew from the Intermediate-Range Nuclear Forces (INF) Treaty with Russia, accusing Russia of violating the treaty by developing intermediate-range missiles. The withdrawal from the treaty marked the end of a key arms control agreement.
4. **United States-Mexico-Canada Agreement (USMCA):** Trump renegotiated NAFTA (North American Free Trade Agreement) and achieved the United States-Mexico-Canada Agreement (USMCA) in 2018. This revised agreement focused on issues such as automobile trade, intellectual property, and agricultural market access.
5. **Strategic Nuclear Arms Treaty (START):** Although initially critical of the START Treaty with Russia, Trump extended the agreement in 2020 before its expiration. START limits the number of strategic nuclear weapons deployed by the United States and Russia.
6. **Trans-Pacific Partnership (TPP):** In one of his first acts as president, Trump withdrew the United States from the TPP, a trade agreement that would have united 12 Pacific nations. He argued that this agreement was not beneficial for the United States.
7. **Open Skies Treaty:** In 2020, Trump announced the intention to withdraw from the Open Skies Treaty, which allowed participating countries to conduct aerial observation flights over other countries' territories to promote transparency and mutual trust.

In addition to withdrawing from international treaties and agreements, Trump also signed some new agreements, including:

- The Abraham Accords: Trump negotiated a series of agreements to normalize relations between Israel and Arab countries, including the United Arab Emirates, Bahrain, Sudan, and Morocco.
- The U.S.-Israel Peace Agreement: Trump also negotiated a peace agreement between the United States and Israel, which included the normalization of relations between Israel and the United Arab Emirates.
- The United States-Mexico-Canada Agreement (USMCA): Trump negotiated a new trade agreement between the United States, Mexico, and Canada, which replaced NAFTA.

Trump's policies regarding international treaties and agreements were criticized for isolating the United States from the world and damaging its relationships with allies. However, Trump also achieved some accomplishments, such as the partial denuclearization of North Korea and the signing of new trade agreements with Mexico, Canada, and Japan.

Policy towards China, Russia, the European Union, and Latin America

The policy of the Trump administration towards China, Russia, the European Union, and Latin America was marked by diverse and sometimes conflicting approaches. Below is a detailed account of the policy towards each of these regions:

1. **Policy towards China:** The relationship with China was one of the most prominent aspects of Trump's foreign policy. His approach focused on several key points:

- **Trade war:** Trump initiated a trade war with China, imposing tariffs on billions of dollars of Chinese products and accusing China of unfair trade practices and intellectual property theft.
- **Trade relations**: He sought a trade agreement with China, which materialized in "Phase 1" of the U.S.-China trade agreement in January 2020. This agreement included commitments from China to increase its purchases of U.S. products.
- **Tensions in the South China Sea:** The Trump administration expressed concerns about Chinese military expansion in the South China Sea and conducted freedom of navigation operations to challenge Chinese territorial claims.
- **Technology and national security**: Trump also focused his attention on technology and national security issues related to China, including restrictions on Chinese companies such as Huawei and the video application TikTok.

1. **Policy towards Russia:** The relationship with Russia was a subject of debate and controversy during Trump's tenure:

- **Interference in the 2016 elections:** Russian interference in the 2016 elections was a matter of concern. Although Trump expressed skepticism about this interference, his administration took measures, such as sanctions, against Russian individuals and entities.
- Relationship with Putin: Trump sought a closer relationship with Russian President Vladimir Putin. He held meetings with Putin on several occasions, which generated criticism and concerns about the lack of transparency in these summits.
- Nuclear weapons: The Trump administration extended the START Treaty with Russia before its expiration and explored the possibility of a new arms control agreement.

1. **Policy towards the European Union:** The relationship with the European Union was marked by tensions on several fronts:

- **Trade:** Trump expressed criticism towards the European Union on trade issues and threatened to impose tariffs on European products, especially related to the automotive industry.
- **NATO:** He questioned the commitment of some NATO members to defense spending and demanded that they increase their financial contributions.
- **Iran nuclear deal (JCPOA):** While the European Union supported the JCPOA, Trump withdrew from the agreement and reimposed sanctions on Iran, generating tensions with Europe.

1. **Policy towards Latin America:** The policy towards Latin America focused largely on immigration and trade relations:

- **Immigration:** Trump implemented stricter immigration policies, including family separation at the border with Mexico and the cancellation of the DACA program.
- Trade: He renegotiated the North American Free Trade Agreement (NAFTA), which became the United States-Mexico-Canada Agreement (USMCA). He also imposed tariffs on Mexican and Brazilian products.
- **Venezuela:** Trump led international efforts to pressure the government of Nicolás Maduro in Venezuela and recognize opposition leader Juan Guaidó as interim president.

Trump's policy towards these regions was in line with his "America First" approach and generated a variety of reactions and challenges both domestically and internationally.

EGOCENTRISM AND POLITICS IN THE TRUMP ERA

Chapter 5: The Second Campaign and the 2020 Election

The political history of the United States was once again filled with anticipation as the year 2020 approached. Donald Trump's first term had been a whirlwind of controversies, disruptive policies, and international challenges. Now, facing the possibility of a second term, Trump embarked on a re-election campaign that would be one of the most intensely watched and debated in modern U.S. history.

In this chapter, we will explore in detail how Trump's re-election campaign unfolded in the midst of a deeply divided country. We will examine the campaign strategies, Trump's speeches, his debates with Democratic candidate Joe Biden, and the key political events that defined this historic election.

The 2020 election was not only a political showdown between two candidates, but it also took place in the midst of the COVID-19 pandemic, which led to significant changes in how the campaign was conducted and in the voting itself. The use of mail-in voting, tensions over election security, and controversy surrounding the results marked this electoral process.

In this chapter, we will also explore how the 2020 election became a referendum on Trump's leadership style, his handling of the pandemic, and the political divisions in the United States. As we progress through this narrative, we will analyze the election results and how Trump accepted or challenged the results, culminating in significant events such as the assault on the U.S. Capitol on January 6, 2021.

Donald Trump's Second Campaign and the 2020 Election left an indelible mark on U.S. political history, and this chapter will immerse us in the key moments and political dynamics that defined this crucial period in Trump's presidency.

Announcement of Re-election

The announcement of Donald Trump's re-election as President of the United States was a crucial moment in American politics and a milestone in his presidency. Below is a description of how this announcement took place:

Re-election Announcement (June 18, 2019):

On June 18, 2019, Donald Trump officially announced his intention to seek re-election as President of the United States in the 2020 election. He did so at a campaign rally in Orlando, Florida, where thousands of supporters gathered to hear his announcement.

In his announcement speech, Trump highlighted his achievements during his first term, including tax reform, deregulation, and strengthening the economy. He also addressed issues such as immigration, border security, and his "America First" approach. Trump presented his campaign as an effort to "keep America great" and promised to address challenges such as illegal immigration, trade, and the fight against terrorism.

Trump's re-election campaign slogan was "Keep America Great," a continuation of his 2016 campaign slogan, "Make America Great Again."

Trump's re-election announcement marked the beginning of an intense political campaign that lasted for the next year and a half until the November 2020 presidential election. During that time, Trump focused on mobilizing his base of supporters and competing against several Democratic candidates in the primary elections, including the eventual Democratic nominee, Joe Biden. The 2020 election became a crucial referendum on Trump's presidency and his policies.

Campaign Development

EGOCENTRISM AND POLITICS IN THE TRUMP ERA

The development of Donald Trump's 2020 re-election campaign was a complex and highly observed political process that involved a series of strategies and key events. Here are some highlights of his campaign development:

1. Communication Strategy:

• Campaign rallies: Trump held a series of campaign rallies across the country, which became a hallmark of his strategy. These events attracted enthusiastic crowds and allowed him to connect directly with his base of supporters.

• Use of social media: Trump continued to use Twitter and other social media to communicate directly with his followers and convey campaign messages. His tweets often generated media attention and debate.

• TV and digital advertising: Trump's campaign invested significantly in television and digital platform advertising, especially in key states.

2. Campaign Themes:

• Economy: Trump highlighted his pre-pandemic economic record, arguing that he had presided over strong economic growth and low unemployment before the COVID-19 crisis.

• Immigration: He continued to focus on immigration, promising stricter policies and the construction of a border wall.

• Law and Order: In response to protests and riots that erupted across the country, Trump emphasized "law and order" and promised to maintain security and law enforcement.

• Judicial appointments: Trump highlighted his nominations of conservative judges to federal courts, including the Supreme Court.

3. National Conventions:

• Republican National Convention: Due to the COVID-19 pandemic, the 2020 Republican National Convention was largely virtual. Trump accepted his nomination from the White House and presented his vision for America under his leadership.

4. Democratic Primary Elections:
- During the Democratic primary elections, Trump and his campaign closely observed the process and attacked several of the Democratic candidates, ultimately focusing on Joe Biden as his rival.

5. Challenges and Controversies:
- The COVID-19 pandemic presented a significant challenge for the campaign, as rallies and campaign events had to be adapted or canceled due to public health restrictions.
- Trump generated controversy by questioning the legitimacy of mail-in voting and expressing concerns about potential electoral fraud.

6. Presidential Debates:
- Trump participated in three presidential debates with Joe Biden, where key issues were discussed and accusations and criticisms were exchanged.

7. Election and Post-election:
- The presidential election took place on November 3, 2020. As votes were counted, Trump contested the results in several key states, arguing without evidence that there had been electoral fraud.
- The certification of the electoral results in Congress on January 6, 2021, culminated in an assault on the Capitol by Trump supporters, which led to Trump's suspension from Twitter and other social media platforms.

Trump's 2020 campaign development can be divided into the following stages:
- Stage 1: Campaign Launch (2019-2020)
- Trump announced his re-election bid on June 18, 2019. In the following months, Trump traveled across the country holding rallies and fundraising events. He also launched a series of television and radio ads.
- Trump campaigned with a message of unity and prosperity. He promised to create jobs, improve the economy, and protect U.S.

borders. He also criticized Biden for his age, his past, and his alleged lack of experience.

- Stage 2: COVID-19 Pandemic (2020)
- In March 2020, the COVID-19 pandemic spread across the United States. Trump was criticized for his handling of the pandemic, which resulted in the death of over 200,000 Americans.
- Trump refused to take strict measures to contain the spread of the virus. He also criticized Democratic governors for their efforts to impose restrictions.
- Stage 3: Death of George Floyd (2020)
- In May 2020, the death of George Floyd at the hands of Minneapolis police sparked protests for racial justice across the United States. Trump was criticized for his response to the protests, which was perceived as authoritarian and divisive.
- Trump sent federal forces to cities to suppress the protests. He also used force to clear protesters from Lafayette Square, in front of the White House.
- Stage 4: Presidential Elections (2020)
- The presidential election was held on November 3, 2020. Biden won the popular vote by a margin of over 7 million votes. He also won the electoral vote by 306 to 232, giving him victory in the election.
- Trump rejected the election results and accused Biden of electoral fraud. He filed a series of lawsuits to contest the results, but all were dismissed.
- The Biden administration took over on January 20, 2021. Trump left the White House and became the first U.S. president to be banned from Twitter.

Overall, Trump's second campaign was a failure. He failed to win re-election, and his rejection of the election results created a great division in the country.

Despite Trump's and his campaign's efforts to contest the results, Joe Biden was declared the winner of the 2020 presidential election and assumed the presidency on January 20, 2021. Trump's 2020 campaign was one of the most controversial and intense chapters in U.S. political history.

2020 Presidential Election and Its Results

The 2020 presidential election in the United States was one of the most significant and controversial political events in recent history of the country.

Biden won the popular vote by a margin of over 7 million votes, and also won the electoral vote by 306 to 232. It was the first time a Democratic candidate had won the presidency without winning the state of Florida since Franklin D. Roosevelt in 1932.

Trump rejected the election results and accused Biden of electoral fraud. He filed a series of lawsuits to contest the results, but all were dismissed.

The Biden administration took over on January 20, 2021. Trump left the White House and became the first U.S. president to be banned from Twitter.

Here are the key aspects of this election and its results:

Main Candidates:

- Donald Trump (Republican): Sought re-election as President of the United States. He headed the Republican Party ticket.

- Joe Biden (Democrat): Was the Democratic candidate and ran in an effort to challenge Trump's presidency.

Election Results:

- The presidential election was held on November 3, 2020.

- Joe Biden won the presidential election and became the 46th President of the United States.

- Biden obtained 306 electoral votes, while Trump obtained 232 electoral votes.

- Biden also won the popular vote, receiving over 81 million votes (51.3%) compared to Trump's over 74 million votes (46.8%).

Controversy and Challenges:

EGOCENTRISM AND POLITICS IN THE TRUMP ERA

- The 2020 election was marked by a series of controversies and legal challenges promoted by the Trump campaign. They alleged electoral fraud and filed lawsuits in several key states.
- These legal challenges were reviewed and rejected by numerous courts across the country, which found no evidence of widespread fraud that affected the outcome of the election.

Certification in Congress:

- On January 6, 2021, Congress met to certify the electoral results. During this session, Trump supporters stormed the U.S. Capitol in an attempt to stop the certification process. This event was strongly condemned by leaders of both parties and resulted in the death of several people.
- Despite the interruption of the process, Congress eventually certified the electoral results, ratifying Joe Biden's victory.
- On January 20, 2021, Joe Biden officially assumed the presidency of the United States in an inauguration ceremony in Washington, D.C.

The following are some of the factors that contributed to Trump's defeat in 2020:

- The COVID-19 pandemic: Trump was criticized for his handling of the pandemic, which resulted in the death of over 200,000 Americans.
- The economy: The U.S. economy was negatively affected by the pandemic, and Trump was criticized for not doing enough to help those affected.
- Trump's leadership style: Trump was criticized for his leadership style, which was perceived as authoritarian and divisive.
- Biden's appeal: Biden was a more moderate candidate than Trump and was perceived as a candidate more capable of uniting the country.

The 2020 presidential election and subsequent events were highly divisive and generated intense political and legal debate in the United

States. Although there were disputes and controversies, the final results confirmed the election of Joe Biden as president.

Chapter 6: The Unachieved Second Term and the End of the Presidency

As the 2020 presidential election came to a close, attention focused on whether Donald Trump would secure a second term in the White House or if Joe Biden would take the presidency. Despite a fierce campaign effort and a fervent base of supporters, Trump faced an electoral defeat that generated unprecedented controversies and legal challenges.

Trump's defeat was a surprise to many, as he had been a popular president during his first term. However, a series of factors contributed to his loss, including the COVID-19 pandemic, the economy, and his leadership style.

The COVID-19 pandemic was a major factor in Trump's defeat. He was criticized for his handling of the pandemic, which resulted in the deaths of more than 200,000 Americans.

The economy also played a significant role in Trump's defeat. The U.S. economy was negatively impacted by the pandemic, and Trump was criticized for not doing enough to help those affected.

In this chapter, we will explore the key events surrounding Trump's attempt to secure a second term and how he responded to the election results. We will examine the controversies, legal challenges, and allegations of electoral fraud that emerged, as well as the certification of the results in Congress and the storming of the Capitol that shocked the nation.

We will also consider how Trump handled his exit from the presidency and his relationship with incoming President Joe Biden.

The peaceful transfer of power is a fundamental feature of American democracy, and this period was a critical test of that tradition.

Ultimately, Trump's unachieved second term and the end of his presidency highlighted the political division and polarization in the United States. This period of transition and transfer of power was a pivotal moment in the country's history, and its effects continue to resonate in American politics and society.

Post-Election Controversies

The post-election controversies following the 2020 U.S. presidential election were a dominant theme in the country's politics and society. These controversies largely centered around allegations of electoral fraud and attempts by Donald Trump's campaign and his supporters to challenge the election results. Below are some of the main post-election controversies:

1. **Allegations of Electoral Fraud**:
    - Trump's campaign and its allies made numerous allegations of electoral fraud in several key states. They argued that irregularities occurred in the voting process, including issues with mail-in voting and vote counting.
    - These allegations were presented in the form of lawsuits in several states, seeking to overturn the results or hold new elections.
    - Despite these claims, multiple courts and election officials in various states found no evidence of widespread electoral fraud that could change the outcome of the election.
2. **Vote Recounts and Audits**:
    - In some states, vote recounts and audits were conducted to verify the accuracy of the election results. These recounts largely confirmed Joe Biden's

victory.
- Michigan, Wisconsin, Georgia, and other states conducted audits and recounts that found no significant irregularities.

3. **Storming of the Capitol**:
   - The storming of the U.S. Capitol on January 6, 2021, was a climactic moment in the post-election controversies. A mob of Trump supporters stormed the Capitol in an attempt to stop the certification of Biden's victory.
   - The Capitol attack was a violent assault on American democracy. It was also an attack on the national security of the United States.

4. **Certification of Results in Congress**:
   - On January 6, 2021, Congress convened to certify the electoral results in a joint session. During this session, Trump supporters stormed the U.S. Capitol in an attempt to halt the certification process.
   - Despite the chaos and disruption, Congress ultimately certified the results, ratifying Joe Biden's victory.

5. **Loss of Social Media Access**:
   - Following the events of January 6 and due to his allegations of electoral fraud, Donald Trump was suspended from social media platforms such as Twitter and Facebook. These suspensions sparked debates about online freedom of speech.

6. **Transfer of Power**:
   - On January 20, 2021, Joe Biden was officially sworn in as President of the United States in an inauguration ceremony in Washington, D.C.
   - The transfer of power took place peacefully, though

it was marked by unprecedented tensions and challenges.

These post-election controversies and efforts to challenge the election results were a dominant theme in American politics in the aftermath of the 2020 election. While the allegations of electoral fraud were widely dismissed by courts and election officials, they generated significant divisions in the country and contributed to the political polarization that continues to affect the United States.

Legal Challenges and Protests

The 2020 U.S. presidential election was one of the most contested in the country's history. Joe Biden's victory over Donald Trump was narrow, and Trump did not accept the election results.

Trump and his allies alleged electoral fraud but provided no credible evidence to support their claims. They filed a series of lawsuits to contest the results, but all were dismissed.

Trump's allegations of electoral fraud were rejected by election officials, courts, and the media. They were also rejected by most Americans, according to polls.

Trump's claims were widely criticized as an attempt to undermine American democracy. They were also seen as an attack on Biden's legitimacy as president.

Here are the key aspects of the legal challenges and protests:

1. **Legal Challenges**:
    - Trump's reelection campaign and its allies filed a series of legal challenges in several key states, alleging electoral fraud or irregularities in the voting process.
    - These lawsuits sought to contest the election results and, in some cases, requested the annulment of votes or the holding of new elections.
    - The vast majority of these lawsuits were dismissed by state and federal courts due to a lack of solid evidence

of widespread electoral fraud that could change the election outcome. Some judges expressed concern over the lack of concrete evidence in the lawsuits.

2. **Protests and Marches**:
    - Following the election, protests and marches were held in several U.S. cities. Some of these protests were organized by Trump supporters and centered on allegations of electoral fraud.
    - In Washington, D.C., thousands of Trump supporters gathered for a rally known as the "Freedom March" on December 12, 2020. The rally culminated in clashes with police and arrests.
    - On January 6, 2021, a rally in support of Trump turned into the storming of the U.S. Capitol by a mob of his supporters, resulting in deaths and significant damage. This was one of the most notable and controversial protests of this period.

3. **Vote Recounts and Audits**:
    - In response to fraud allegations, vote recounts and audits were conducted in several key states. These recounts and audits largely confirmed the original results.
    - Michigan, Wisconsin, Georgia, and other states conducted review processes that found no significant irregularities.

4. **Certification of Results in Congress**:
    - On January 6, 2021, Congress convened to certify the electoral results in a joint session. During this session, Trump supporters stormed the U.S. Capitol in an attempt to stop the certification process.
    - Despite the chaos and interruption, Congress ultimately certified the results, ratifying Joe Biden's

victory.
5. **Impact:**
    - The post-election controversies of 2020 had a lasting impact on American politics. They left Americans divided over the country's future and undermined confidence in democratic institutions.
    - Trump's allegations of electoral fraud fueled distrust in the U.S. electoral system. They also led to greater political polarization, as Trump's supporters refused to accept the election results.
    - The storming of the Capitol was a moment of crisis for American democracy. It was a reminder that democracy is fragile and must be protected.
    - The post-election controversies of 2020 also had an impact on global politics. They showed that American democracy is not immune to internal threats and that even an established democracy can be vulnerable to manipulation and misinformation.

These legal challenges and protests following the 2020 election generated intense controversy in the United States and contributed to the political polarization in the country. Despite efforts to contest the results, Joe Biden assumed the presidency of the United States on January 20, 2021, and the transfer of power took place peacefully.

Transition to the Biden Administration

The transition to the Biden administration began on November 7, 2020, the day after the 2020 presidential election. The U.S. General Services Administration (GSA) announced that day that it would formally recognize Biden's transition, allowing him access to funds and assistance to begin organizing his government.

Biden's transition team quickly formed and began working on a variety of tasks, including selecting nominees for cabinet positions, crafting a plan to address the country's most pressing issues, and preparing for Biden's inauguration on January 20, 2021.

One of the first tasks of the transition team was selecting nominees for cabinet positions. Biden wanted to form a diverse cabinet that represented the different voices and perspectives of the United States. The transition team reviewed thousands of resumes and interviewed hundreds of candidates before presenting the final nominations to Biden.

The transition team also worked on crafting a plan to address the country's most urgent issues. These issues included the COVID-19 pandemic, the economy, racial justice, and climate change. The transition team developed a series of proposals to tackle these problems, which Biden presented in his acceptance speech.

Below are the key aspects of this transition:

1. **Joe Biden's Election**:
    - Joe Biden was declared the winner of the presidential election on November 7, 2020, after media outlets projected that he had won enough states to secure a majority in the Electoral College.
    - Biden won 306 electoral votes, surpassing the 270 needed to win, and received more than 81 million popular votes, the highest number ever recorded in a U.S. presidential election.
2. **Preparations for the Inauguration**:
    - Joe Biden's presidential inauguration was scheduled for January 20, 2021. Preparations for the event included organizing a swearing-in ceremony and a series of related activities.
3. **Transition Cooperation**:
    - Despite the post-election controversies, Donald Trump's administration and his team began to

cooperate in the transition to Biden's incoming administration.
- The General Services Administration (GSA) formally authorized the transition on November 23, 2020, allowing Biden's team to access resources and funds necessary for the governmental transition.

4. **Speeches and Messages of Unity**:
   - Both Joe Biden and Donald Trump delivered speeches calling for unity and healing the nation's divisions. Biden emphasized the need to work together amid the challenges, including the COVID-19 pandemic.

5. **Presidential Inauguration**:
   - Joe Biden's inauguration as the 46th president of the United States took place on January 20, 2021, at the U.S. Capitol in Washington, D.C. Due to the COVID-19 pandemic and security concerns, the ceremony was held in a more limited format with social distancing measures in place.
   - In his inauguration speech, Biden called for unity and urged Americans to overcome divisions and work together to tackle the country's challenges.

6. **Change of Government**:
   - After the swearing-in ceremony, the transition of power began and Biden's administration took office. This included the appointment of cabinet members and other key officials.

7. **Biden Administration Policies and Priorities**:
   - The Biden administration focused on a range of key issues and challenges, including the response to the COVID-19 pandemic, economic recovery, climate change, immigration reform, and promoting unity

and racial justice.

The transition to the Biden administration marked a significant shift in the political direction and policy priorities of the United States. The peaceful transfer of power is a cornerstone of American democracy, and the transition process was a testament to the resilience and stability of the country's democratic institutions.

Conspiracy Theories About Biden's Election

Conspiracy theories about Joe Biden's election as president of the United States in 2020 are a series of false beliefs that allege the election was fraudulent and that Biden did not legitimately win.

These theories have been promoted by former President Donald Trump and his allies and have been widely rejected by election officials, courts, and the media.

During and after the 2020 U.S. presidential election, several conspiracy theories emerged related to Joe Biden's victory. These theories were based on unfounded claims and misinformation and were widely debunked by experts and election officials. Some of the most prominent conspiracy theories included:

1. **Widespread Electoral Fraud**:
    - This theory claimed that the 2020 election was marred by widespread electoral fraud that affected results in multiple states. Unfounded claims of fraudulent ballots and vote manipulation were widely circulated.
2. **"QAnon" and the "Big Steal"**:
    - Supporters of the "QAnon" conspiracy theory promoted the idea that there was a secret plan to steal the election from Trump and that this plan was part of a battle against a pedophile and satanic elite.
3. **Dominion Voting Machines**:
    - The false claim was spread that voting machines

manufactured by Dominion Voting Systems were designed to manipulate electoral results in favor of Joe Biden.

4. **Vote Switching Conspiracy Theories**:
    - Some argued that Trump's votes were systematically switched to votes for Biden through software manipulation or malfunctioning voting machines.
5. **Claims of "Contested" States**:
    - It was claimed that key battleground states, such as Georgia, Michigan, and Pennsylvania, were subject to widespread fraud that changed the results in favor of Biden.

It is important to emphasize that these conspiracy theories were not supported by solid evidence nor confirmed by independent election officials or courts. The 2020 election was reviewed and audited in several states, and no evidence of widespread electoral fraud that could have altered the results was found. The peaceful transfer of power proceeded, and Joe Biden assumed the presidency of the United States on January 20, 2021.

.

Chapter 7: Donald Trump's Legacy

Donald Trump's presidency was, without a doubt, one of the most unusual and controversial in U.S. history. From his election in 2016 until the end of his term in 2021, Trump left an indelible mark on American politics and culture. His policies and approaches generated deep divisions in the country, and his unique and unprecedented leadership style attracted both passionate support and intense criticism.

In this chapter, we will explore Donald Trump's legacy from various perspectives. We will examine his key achievements and policies, including tax reform, judicial nominations, immigration policies, and the response to the COVID-19 pandemic. We will also consider how his "America First" approach impacted international relations and the United States' position in the world.

In addition to his policies and actions in office, we will discuss Trump's impact on American politics and the transformation of his party, the Republican Party. We will also analyze his influence on political rhetoric, social media, and polarization.

Donald Trump's legacy remains a subject of ongoing debate and discussion, and this chapter seeks to provide a comprehensive view of his presidency and its lasting impact on U.S. politics and society.

Impact on U.S. Politics

Donald Trump's impact on U.S. politics was profound and enduring. During his presidency, Trump significantly transformed the political landscape and left a lasting imprint on his party, the

Republican Party, as well as on the political system as a whole. Here are some of the key aspects of his impact on U.S. politics:

1. **Transformation of the Republican Party:**
   - Trump redefined the Republican Party in his image. His leadership style and his nationalist and populist political approach influenced the direction of the party.
   - Republicans who were critical of or challenged Trump faced the possibility of opposition from his loyal base of supporters.
   - Trump's influence on the party led to a stronger alignment with his approach to issues such as immigration, trade, and foreign policy.
2. **Mobilization of the Support Base:**
   - Trump mobilized a passionate and committed base of supporters, resulting in high voter turnout in both primary and presidential elections.
   - His direct communication style through social media, particularly Twitter, allowed him to effectively connect with his base and shape the political narrative.
3. **Polarization and Division:**
   - Trump's presidency exacerbated political polarization in the United States. His policies and rhetoric often deepened divisions between Democrats and Republicans.
   - Trump's aggressive and confrontational tone in politics and his clashes with the press contributed to a highly polarized political atmosphere.
4. **Judicial Appointments:**
   - One of Trump's most lasting legacies was his

influence on the nomination of federal judges and the confirmation of three justices to the Supreme Court, shifting the ideological balance of the court.
- These appointments secured a conservative majority on the Supreme Court, significantly impacting important legal decisions.

5. **Communication Style and Social Media:**
   - Trump set a new standard for presidential communication through his active and often controversial use of social media.
   - His Twitter account became a powerful tool for communicating directly with the public and expressing his opinions and policies.

6. **Breaking Norms and Conventions:**
   - Trump's presidency was characterized by a break from established political norms and conventions. His nontraditional leadership style challenged expectations of the presidency.
   - Trump questioned the validity of the election, which resulted in the storming of the Capitol by his supporters after the 2020 election.

7. **Changes in Law and Policy:**
   - Trump succeeded in passing a series of laws and policies that advanced his political agenda. These included the 2017 Tax Cuts and Jobs Act, the construction of a border wall between the United States and Mexico, and the withdrawal of the U.S. from the Paris Agreement on climate change.

8. **Undermining Confidence in Democratic Institutions:**
   - Trump repeatedly attacked U.S. democratic institutions, including the media, the judiciary, and the electoral system. His attacks eroded trust in these

institutions for many Americans.

Donald Trump's impact on U.S. politics continues to be a subject of debate and discussion, and his legacy will continue to influence the political dynamics of the United States in the years to come. His disruptive political style and his ability to mobilize a loyal base make him a significant figure in the nation's political history.

Economic Policy and Tax Reforms

Economic policy and tax reforms during Donald Trump's presidency were characterized by an emphasis on deregulation and tax reduction. Below is a summary of some key aspects of Trump's economic policy:

1. **2017 Tax Reform (Tax Cuts and Jobs Act):**
   - One of the main economic policies of the Trump administration was the passage of the Tax Cuts and Jobs Act in 2017. This legislation significantly reduced corporate and personal tax rates.
   - The corporate tax rate was lowered from 35% to 21%, with the aim of stimulating business investment and economic growth.
   - Individual tax rates were reduced for most taxpayers, and the standard deduction was doubled.
2. **Economic Deregulation:**
   - The Trump administration sought to reduce government regulations, arguing that this would encourage investment and economic growth.
   - Steps were taken to reduce regulations in sectors such as energy, the environment, financial services, and healthcare.
3. **Trade Policy:**
   - Trump implemented a more protectionist trade policy, using tariffs to pressure trade partners,

particularly China, in pursuit of more favorable trade deals for the U.S.
- Key trade agreements were renegotiated, such as the United States-Mexico-Canada Agreement (USMCA), which replaced the North American Free Trade Agreement (NAFTA).
4. **Economic Response to the COVID-19 Pandemic:**
    - During the COVID-19 pandemic, the Trump administration implemented an economic stimulus package known as the CARES Act, which provided direct payments to citizens, business assistance, and support for workers affected by the crisis.
    - The Federal Reserve also implemented policies of quantitative easing and interest rate cuts to stimulate the economy.
5. **Economic Growth and Employment:**
    - Prior to the pandemic, the economy experienced a period of solid growth, and the unemployment rate fell to historically low levels.
    - However, the COVID-19 pandemic had a significant impact on the economy, leading to an economic recession.

The Trump administration's economic policy sparked significant debate. Supporters argued that the tax reforms and deregulation boosted economic growth before the pandemic, while critics questioned the fairness of the tax cuts and argued that trade tensions could have long-term negative effects on the economy.

It is important to note that the evaluation of the long-term impact of Trump's economic policy remains a subject of debate and study, and the long-term economic effects may require more time to be fully assessed.

Immigration Policy and Border Security

Donald Trump's immigration and border security policy was one of the most controversial aspects of his presidency. Trump made reducing illegal immigration one of his top priorities, and he adopted a series of measures to achieve this goal.

One of Trump's most controversial measures was the construction of a border wall between the United States and Mexico. Trump promised to build a 1,900-mile-long concrete wall along the U.S.-Mexico border. Construction of the wall began in 2017, but it remains unfinished.

Below is a summary of key aspects of the Trump administration's immigration and border security policy:

1. **Border Wall Construction**:
    - One of Trump's signature campaign promises was the construction of a wall on the U.S.-Mexico border to strengthen security.
    - The Trump administration worked on the construction and expansion of the border wall throughout his term, although much of the infrastructure already existed in the form of fences and barriers.
2. **"Zero Tolerance" Policy and Family Separation**:
    - In 2018, the administration implemented a "zero tolerance" policy that resulted in the separation of migrant families at the border. This policy generated intense controversy and was later reversed in response to public outrage.
3. **Changes to DACA Status**:
    - The Deferred Action for Childhood Arrivals (DACA) program, which protects certain undocumented young immigrants from deportation,

was the subject of changes and legal challenges during the Trump administration.
- The administration sought to end DACA, but the U.S. Supreme Court blocked those efforts in June 2020.

4. **Asylum Policy and Migrant Protection Protocols (MPP):**
    - The Trump administration implemented stricter policies to limit asylum applications and required some asylum seekers to wait in Mexico while their cases were processed, known as the Migrant Protection Protocols (MPP).
    - These policies aimed to reduce migration across the southern U.S. border.

5. **Restrictions on Legal Immigration:**
    - The administration also implemented restrictions on legal immigration, including reducing the number of refugees admitted and imposing restrictions on the issuance of visas and green cards.

6. **Increased Deportations:**
    - Deportations of undocumented immigrants increased during Trump's presidency, although they primarily focused on those with criminal records.

Trump's immigration and border security policy generated intense debate in the United States. His supporters argued that these measures were necessary to protect the country's security and sovereignty, while his critics argued that they were inhumane and undermined American values of inclusiveness and hospitality. Trump's immigration policy left a lasting and controversial impact on U.S. politics and society.

Repercussions in the Republican Party

Donald Trump's presidency had a significant impact on the Republican Party. Trump transformed the party, shifting it to the right and making it more populist and nationalist.

Before Trump, the Republican Party was more moderate, with a more diverse voter base. However, Trump appealed to white, conservative, and nationalist voters and succeeded in mobilizing this base to vote for him.

Trump's presidency also led to a division within the Republican Party. Some Republicans opposed Trump's policies and actions, while others supported him unconditionally. This division persists to this day and is likely to continue in future elections.

Here are some of the main repercussions that Trump's presidency had on the Republican Party:

1. **Ideological Reconfiguration**:
    - Trump redefined the Republican Party's ideological identity by promoting a populist and nationalist approach instead of traditional conservatism.
    - This approach included more protectionist policies on trade, a tougher stance on immigration, and a less interventionist approach to foreign policy.
2. **Loyalty to Trump**:
    - During his presidency, Trump consolidated a loyal base of supporters within the Republican Party. His charismatic leadership style and ability to mobilize voters created a deeply committed base to his leadership.
    - Republicans who expressed criticism or disagreements with Trump often faced resistance from the base and the possibility of primary election challenges.
3. **Internal Polarization**:

- Trump's presidency exacerbated polarization within the Republican Party. Divisions became evident between those who firmly supported Trump and those who maintained a more traditional perspective of the party.
- Party tensions were evident on issues such as immigration policy, trade, and relations with international leaders.

4. **Judicial Appointments**:
    - One of Trump's most lasting legacies was his influence on the nomination of federal judges, including three Supreme Court justices. These appointments consolidated a conservative majority on the Supreme Court, a significant issue for conservative Republicans.

5. **Rhetoric and Political Style**:
    - Trump introduced a politically incorrect communication style and rhetoric into the party, challenging political conventions and political correctness.
    - His active use of social media, particularly Twitter, allowed him to communicate directly with the base and shape the political narrative.

6. **Challenges to the Republican Establishment**:
    - Trump challenged the old guard of the Republican Party, including long-established leaders and political figures. This led to a reconfiguration of the party's direction.

In summary, Donald Trump's presidency left a profound mark on the Republican Party, transforming its ideological identity and internal dynamics. Loyalty to Trump and his influence within the party remain central issues in current Republican politics, and the party's future will continue to be a subject of debate and evolution.

Chapter 8: Donald Trump's Style and Personality

Donald Trump's presidency was characterized not only by his policies and decisions but also by his distinctive style and unique personality in contemporary American politics. From his communicative approach on social media to his frank rhetoric and ability to attract a passionate base of followers, Trump challenged traditional expectations of presidential leadership.

In this chapter, we will explore Donald Trump's style and personality in depth. We will analyze how his communication style, which often included provocative tweets and direct comments, impacted American politics and culture. We will also examine his relationship with the media, which was both tumultuous and highly influential.

Furthermore, we will consider Trump's public image and how his personality influenced the perception of him as a political leader. From his defiant attitude to his focus on loyalty and intuition-driven decision-making, we will evaluate how these characteristics impacted his presidency and his relationship with the public and other leaders.

Donald Trump's style and personality are topics that will continue to be subjects of study and debate in U.S. political history. This chapter seeks to provide a deep insight into how these unique characteristics shaped his presidency and his legacy in the American political landscape.

Communication and Use of Social Media

COMMUNICATION AND THE use of social media played a central role in Donald Trump's presidency and were one of the most distinctive aspects of his leadership style. Here are some of the key elements of his communication and use of social media:

1. **Active Use of Twitter:** • Donald Trump became the first sitting president to actively use Twitter as a platform for direct communication with the public. Through his personal account @realDonaldTrump, Trump issued statements, comments, and policy announcements. • His tweets were often direct, provocative, and controversial, generating wide media coverage and diverse reactions.
2. **Challenge to Presidential Communication Conventions**: • Trump's communication style challenged traditional conventions of presidential communication. He did not hesitate to criticize his political opponents, the media, and public figures through Twitter. • This direct and unfiltered communication allowed him to reach his base of supporters and shape the political narrative without media intermediation.
3. **Generation of Controversies:** • Trump's tweets often generated controversy and media attention. His comments on various topics, from foreign policy to personal matters, often generated passionate reactions. • The constant attention to his Twitter account turned his messages into a recurring topic of conversation in the media and the public sphere.
4. **Use of Social Media for Policy Announcements:** • Trump also used his social media accounts to make important policy announcements and changes in his administration. For example, he announced cabinet changes and foreign policy decisions through Twitter.

5. **Reach and Followers:** • Trump had a loyal follower base on social media. His Twitter account had millions of followers, and his messages had a global reach.
6. **Criticisms and Controversies**: • Although his use of social media provided him with a powerful platform, it also generated criticism, including accusations of misinformation and incitement to violence.
7. **Social Media Suspensions:** • After leaving the presidency, Trump faced temporary or permanent suspensions on social media platforms such as Twitter, Facebook, and YouTube due to concerns about incitement to violence and misinformation.

Trump's active use of social media had a significant impact on American politics and how political leaders communicate with the public. His online communication style challenged established conventions and left a lasting legacy in the sphere of politics and social media.

Relationship with the Media

DONALD TRUMP'S RELATIONSHIP with the media was one of the most tense and tumultuous in recent U.S. presidential history.

Trump began his relationship with the media as a presidential candidate. He often accused the media of being biased and against him. He also accused the media of spreading "fake news."

Once Trump became president, his relationship with the media only worsened. He continued to accuse them of being biased and against him. He also refused to answer their questions, often walking away from press conferences and interviews.

Trump also used social media to attack the media. He posted tweets calling them "fake news" and "enemies of the people." He also tweeted false and misleading information about the media.

Here are some of the key aspects of his relationship with the media:

1. Permanent Conflict: • Trump maintained a constant conflict with the media, which he often labeled as "fake news" and "enemies of the people" • His criticisms of the media were a distinctive feature of his presidency and were often directed at established media outlets such as CNN, The New York Times, and The Washington Post.
2. Use of Defamatory Terms: • Trump used defamatory terms to refer to journalists and news presenters with whom he disagreed, which raised concerns about journalists' safety and the polarized political tone.
3. Direct Communication with the Public: • Trump often avoided traditional media and chose to communicate directly with the public through his social media accounts, especially Twitter. • This strategy allowed him to shape the political narrative and reach his base of supporters directly without intermediaries.
4. Press Conferences: • Trump held regular press conferences, but his relationship with journalists on these occasions often became tense and confrontational.
5. White House Access: • The Trump administration restricted access for some media outlets to events and press conferences, which led to tensions and legal demands.
6. Accusations of Misinformation: • Trump faced criticism for his public statements and social media posts, which were sometimes inaccurate or misleading. This raised concerns about misinformation in the social media era.
7. Changes in Communication Policy: • The Trump administration implemented changes in White House communication policy, including the elimination of daily press briefings at one point.

Trump's relationship with the media was a defining feature of his presidency and generated debates about press freedom and the relationship between the executive power and the fourth estate. His confrontational style and frequent criticisms of the media left a lasting mark on the communication dynamics between the government and the media in the United States.

Leadership Characteristics and Decision-Making Style

DONALD TRUMP'S LEADERSHIP characteristics and decision-making style were central aspects of his presidency and generated significant debates and controversies.

Leadership Characteristics

Trump's leadership characteristics include:

- Authoritarian: Trump was a very authoritarian leader. He didn't like to delegate power and preferred to make decisions by himself.
- Impulsive: Trump was a very impulsive leader. He often made decisions without thinking about the consequences.
- Egocentric: Trump was a very egocentric leader. He believed he was always right and often didn't listen to others.
- Narcissistic: Trump was a very narcissistic leader. He cared more about his image than the good of the country.
- Manipulative: Trump was a very manipulative leader. He used his charisma and power to manipulate others to do what he wanted.

Here are some of the key characteristics of his leadership and decision-making style:

1. Charismatic and Direct Style: • Trump was known for his

charismatic and direct communication style. He spoke frankly and straightforwardly, often using colloquial language that resonated with his base of supporters.
2. Intuition-Based Decision Making: • Trump often made decisions based on his intuition and business experience. He was not known for relying heavily on exhaustive analysis or detailed advice.
3. Focus on Personal Loyalty: • He valued personal loyalty in his team and expected his collaborators to be aligned with his vision and objectives. This led to frequent changes in his cabinet and close advisors.
4. Use of Twitter and Social Media: • Trump actively used Twitter and other social media to communicate directly with the public and shape the political narrative. His tweets were a powerful tool to reach his base of supporters and express his opinions and decisions.
5. Confidence in His Judgment: • Trump often expressed great confidence in his own judgment and experience, which led him to make executive decisions without the approval of advisors or experts.
6. Changes of Direction: • His leadership style sometimes led to changes in policies and decisions, which created uncertainty and challenges in policy implementation.
7. Relations with Congress: • Trump maintained complex relationships with Congress, often pressuring legislators from his own party to support his initiatives.
8. "America First" Policy: • One of the key principles of his leadership was the "America First" policy, which prioritized national interests over international agreements and commitments.
9. Alignment with Support Base: • Trump strived to maintain strong alignment with his base of supporters, which he

considered crucial for his political support and preservation in office.
10. Executive Decisions and Executive Orders: • Trump used executive decisions and executive orders to implement policies without the need for Congressional approval on various issues, including immigration and the environment.

Trump's leadership characteristics and decision-making style had a significant impact on his presidency:

- His authoritarian and egocentric style often led to conflicts with Congress and other world leaders.
- His tendency to make impulsive decisions without thinking about the consequences often led to mistakes and negative consequences.
- His constant change of opinion often led to confusion and a loss of confidence in his leadership.

These leadership characteristics and decision-making style contributed to a presidency marked by polarization and controversy. While some appreciated his direct approach and unconventional style, others criticized him for his lack of predictability and what they considered a lack of respect for established norms and institutions. His legacy as a political leader and his leadership style will continue to be subjects of debate and study in American politics.

.

Chapter 9: Criticisms and Controversies

Donald Trump's presidency was one of the most controversial and divisive in U.S. history. His leadership style and policies often generated criticism and triggered a series of controversies that attracted national and international attention. From his relationships with foreign leaders to his management of the COVID-19 pandemic, President Trump was immersed in a series of heated debates.

In this chapter, we will examine some of the most prominent criticisms and notorious controversies that marked Trump's presidency. This will include aspects such as his international relations and communication style, as well as his response to crucial events such as the COVID-19 pandemic and the Black Lives Matter protests. We will also address the accusations of disinformation and the polarization that surrounded his presidency.

This chapter seeks to provide an impartial and balanced view of the criticisms and controversies that defined Donald Trump's presidency, allowing readers to understand the complexity of his term and its impact on American society and global politics.

Accusations of Inappropriate Behavior

Accusations of inappropriate behavior were a recurring theme during Donald Trump's presidency and generated significant controversies. Here are some of the accusations and events related to inappropriate behavior during his term:

1. Sexual harassment accusations:
- Before his presidency, Donald Trump faced numerous accusations of sexual harassment from several women. These

accusations focused on alleged incidents that occurred in the past, and Trump repeatedly denied the accusations and called them false.

- One of the best-known accusations is that of porn actress Stormy Daniels. Daniels claimed that Trump had paid her $130,000 to keep quiet about a sexual relationship they had in 2006. Trump denied the accusation, but in 2018 an out-of-court settlement was reached in which Daniels received $130,000. In May 2023, a Florida grand jury found Trump guilty of sexual harassment and defamation against Daniels and awarded her $5 million in damages.
- Another well-known accusation is that of columnist E. Jean Carroll. Carroll claimed that Trump had raped her in a Manhattan hotel dressing room in 1995. Trump denied the accusation, but in 2019 a judge ruled that Trump must turn over to Carroll a series of documents that could support her accusation.
- In total, more than 20 women accused Trump of inappropriate behavior. These accusations had a significant impact on Trump's presidency and contributed to his image as a womanizer and misogynist.

2. Access Hollywood tape:

- During the 2016 presidential campaign, a 2005 video was revealed in which Trump made vulgar and sexist comments about women in a private conversation with television host Billy Bush. The video, known as the Access Hollywood tape, generated widespread scandal and led to public apologies from Trump.

3. Accusations of misogynistic behavior:

- Throughout his presidency, Trump was criticized for his rhetoric and comments that some considered misogynistic, including insults and disqualifications towards female politicians and journalists.

4. Accusations of racially insensitive comments:

- Trump also faced accusations of making comments and tweets that some considered insensitive or racist. His comments about Black

Lives Matter protesters, as well as his reaction to events such as the violence in Charlottesville, generated controversy and criticism.

5. Immigration policies and family separation:

- The "zero tolerance" policy and family separation at the border generated widespread criticism, including accusations of cruelty and inappropriate treatment of migrant children and their families.

6. Disinformation and manipulation of facts:

- Trump was criticized for his frequent use of disinformation and false claims in his public statements and on social media, which raised concerns about the manipulation of facts and honesty in presidential communication.

It is important to note that these accusations and controversies generated debates and divergent opinions in American society. Some defended Trump and argued that the accusations were politically motivated or exaggerated, while others considered his actions and comments inappropriate and unacceptable. These events formed an integral part of the political and social dynamics during his presidency and continue to be the subject of analysis and debate.

Impeachment and Political Trial

During his presidency, Donald Trump faced two impeachment processes in the U.S. House of Representatives and two corresponding political trials in the Senate. Here is a summary of both processes:

First Impeachment (2019-2020):

- Cause: The first impeachment process focused on accusations of abuse of power and obstruction of Congress. It was alleged that Trump pressured Ukraine to investigate then-presidential candidate Joe Biden and his son Hunter Biden, while freezing military assistance to Ukraine as part of a possible political retaliation.

- Process: In December 2019, the Democrat-controlled House of Representatives approved two articles of impeachment against Trump, accusing him of abuse of power and obstruction of Congress. The political trial moved to the Senate in January 2020.

- Senate Trial: In February 2020, the Republican-controlled Senate voted to acquit Trump of both charges. The two-thirds majority required to convict the president was not reached, and Trump was acquitted.

Second Impeachment (2021):

- Cause: The second impeachment process was based on accusations of "incitement to insurrection" in relation to the events of January 6, 2021, when Trump supporters stormed the U.S. Capitol in an attempt to stop the certification of Joe Biden's electoral victory.
- Process: The House of Representatives, again controlled by Democrats, approved an article of impeachment against Trump for incitement to insurrection in January 2021, making him the first president in U.S. history to face two political trials.
- Senate Trial: Trump's second political trial began in February 2021, after he had already left the presidency. The Senate voted to acquit Trump of the charge of incitement to insurrection. Although seven Republican senators joined the Democrats to vote in favor of conviction, the required two-thirds majority was not reached.

The political trials against Trump were highly controversial events. They had a significant impact on American politics and contributed to the polarization of the country.

The political trials also had a significant impact on Trump's image. They were seen by many as a sign that Trump was a corrupt and illegitimate president.

The political trials against Trump also had a significant impact on the U.S. impeachment system. They showed that impeachment is a powerful tool that can be used to investigate and judge presidents.

Both impeachment processes were highly polarized and generated intense debates in Congress and throughout the country. Trump became the first president to face two political trials, and the results reflected the deep partisan division in the United States at that time. Although he was acquitted on both occasions, the political trials marked an important chapter in U.S. political history and left a lasting legacy in the public perception of Trump and his presidency.

Civil Society Reactions and Protests

During Donald Trump's presidency, there were a series of civil society reactions and protests that reflected the polarization and diversity of opinions in the United States. Here are some of the main reactions and protests that marked his term:

1. Women's March:

• One of the first and largest acts of protest after Trump's inauguration was the Women's March that took place in January 2017 in Washington, D.C., and in cities across the country and the world.

• The march focused on gender equality, reproductive rights, and other women's issues. It was a massive demonstration that attracted millions of people and marked the beginning of persistent activism during Trump's presidency.

2. Black Lives Matter Protests:

• During his presidency, Donald Trump faced a series of protests related to the Black Lives Matter movement in response to police violence and racial discrimination.

• The protests intensified after the death of George Floyd in May 2020 and spread throughout the country. Trump responded in various ways, including mobilizing the National Guard in some cities and using controversial language to describe the protesters.

3. Protests against immigration policies:

• The Trump administration's immigration policies generated protests across the country, especially in response to family separation at the border and the "zero tolerance" policy.

• Pro-immigrant organizations and activists mobilized against these policies, and demonstrations and vigils were held in support of immigrants and asylum seekers.

4. Protests against environmental policies:

- Environmental groups and climate change advocates also protested against the Trump administration's environmental policies, which included the withdrawal of the United States from the Paris Agreement on climate change.
- The protests focused on environmental preservation and the adoption of more sustainable policies.

5. Protests against COVID-19 restrictions:
- During the COVID-19 pandemic, protests were held in various states against restrictions imposed to contain the spread of the virus.
- Some protesters argued that these restrictions infringed on their individual rights and freedoms, while others supported stricter measures to protect public health.

The protests and civil society actions against Trump had a significant impact on American politics. They helped maintain pressure on Trump and his policies and contributed to the polarization of the country.

The protests also helped bring criticisms of Trump to a wider audience. They showed that there was a significant number of Americans who disagreed with Trump's policies and actions.

Civil society actions also had a significant impact on Trump's image. They showed that Trump did not have the unanimous support of the American people, and that there was a significant number of people who were willing to oppose him.

Judicial Problems

Donald Trump's presidency was marked by a series of judicial problems and legal challenges. Here are some of the most significant judicial problems he faced during his term:

1. Russian Collusion Investigation (Russia and 2016 Elections)

One of the most prominent investigations during Trump's presidency was special counsel Robert Mueller's investigation into Russian interference in the 2016 presidential election and any possible collusion between the Trump campaign and Russia.

- The investigation did not find sufficient evidence to accuse Trump or his team of collusion with Russia, but it identified multiple attempts at Russian interference in the elections.

2. Stormy Daniels Payment Case:

- During the 2016 presidential campaign and after taking office, Trump faced accusations that his lawyer, Michael Cohen, had made an illegal payment to adult film actress Stormy Daniels to silence her alleged relationship with Trump.
- Cohen pleaded guilty to campaign finance violations and other related charges, and claimed he was acting under Trump's orders. Trump denied any wrongdoing.

3. Investigation of Trump's finances:

- Throughout his presidency, there were ongoing investigations into Trump's finances, including his tax returns and his family's businesses.
- Trump became the first president in decades not to make his tax returns public, which generated questions and speculation about his assets and potential conflicts of interest.

4. Accusations of obstruction of justice:

- Robert Mueller's investigation also addressed the question of whether Trump had obstructed justice by attempting to interfere with the investigation. Mueller did not reach a definitive conclusion on obstruction, leaving the decision in the hands of the U.S. Attorney General.
- Attorney General William Barr concluded that there was not enough evidence to charge Trump with obstruction of justice.

5. Accusations of abuse of power in political trials:

- In both impeachment trials he faced in the House of Representatives, Trump was accused of abuse of power. Although he was acquitted on both occasions by the Senate, these accusations left a legacy of controversy and political division.

6. Attack on the United States Capitol:

- Trump is also being investigated by the U.S. Department of Justice for his role in the assault on the U.S. Capitol on January 6, 2021. The investigation is examining whether Trump incited his supporters to carry out the attack. In June 2022, a federal grand jury indicted Trump on two counts of obstruction of justice for his role in the Capitol assault.

These are some of the main judicial problems and legal challenges that Donald Trump faced during his presidency. While some of these cases led to convictions or guilty pleas from people in his circle, Trump in his capacity as president was not convicted or faced criminal charges while in office. Judicial problems were a constant topic of debate and scrutiny during his term and continued to be the subject of attention even after he left the presidency.

Chapter 10: The Capitol Attack (January 6, 2021)

January 6, 2021, will go down in United States history as a day of violence and chaos, a direct assault on democracy. What began as a rally in support of Donald Trump quickly escalated into a violent insurrection against Congress, where enraged crowds stormed the Capitol while lawmakers were in session to certify Joe Biden's victory in the 2020 presidential election.

The assault. After a rally held by Trump near the White House, where he reiterated his baseless accusations of electoral fraud and urged his supporters to "fight like hell" to "take back the country," thousands of demonstrators marched to the Capitol. As they approached, the situation intensified when a group of individuals breached security barriers and forced their way into the building. Capitol police, outnumbered, were unable to contain the mob at that moment.

Protesters entered through windows and doors, vandalizing offices and looting the historic building while chanting slogans like "Stop the Steal." Some carried Confederate flags, a symbol of rebellion and white supremacy, while others wore combat gear or even tactical equipment. The scene inside the Capitol turned into absolute chaos. Lawmakers, who were in the middle of certifying the electoral results, were quickly evacuated to secure locations while the intruders roamed the hallways searching for them.

Deaths and injuries. The assault on the Capitol was not only a symbolic attack, but it also had a very real human toll. During the riots, five people lost their lives, including a Capitol police officer, Brian

Sicknick, who died from injuries sustained during confrontations with the protesters. Ashli Babbitt, a fervent Trump supporter and Air Force veteran, was shot dead by a security officer as she attempted to breach a door leading to a restricted area inside the Capitol.

Three other individuals, part of the crowd, died of medical emergencies during the assault, leading to greater scrutiny over the authorities' preparedness and response. In addition to the deaths, more than 140 law enforcement officers were injured, many severely. These officers endured unimaginable brutality while trying to protect the Capitol; some were beaten with metal bars, pepper-sprayed, and subjected to prolonged physical assaults.

The response of the authorities. For several hours, chaos reigned at the Capitol as images of the assault circulated on media outlets and social networks, shocking the world. As the number of protesters grew, it became evident that the initially deployed security forces were unprepared for a crowd this large or for the level of violence that erupted. Only after the National Guard was activated and reinforcements from other security agencies were sent did order begin to be restored.

Immediate repercussions. That same night, despite the attack, Congress reconvened, this time under reinforced security, and certified Joe Biden's electoral victory. The assault left an open wound in American democracy, with many questioning how such violence could reach one of the nation's most emblematic buildings.

Subsequent investigations revealed that the attack was organized by various extremist groups that supported Trump, including the Proud Boys, Oath Keepers, and other white nationalist groups. The FBI and other federal agencies launched a massive operation to identify and arrest those responsible for the attack, resulting in hundreds of arrests over the following weeks and months.

Trump's involvement and conspiracy theories. One of the most controversial aspects of the Capitol attack was Donald Trump's direct involvement. Many of his critics, both inside and outside the United States, accused him of inciting the attack with his incendiary rhetoric and his persistent refusal to accept the results of the 2020 election. For weeks leading up to the attack, Trump had spread conspiracy theories that claimed, without evidence, that the election had been stolen through massive fraud. These claims were dismissed by multiple courts and election oversight bodies but fostered an atmosphere of distrust among his most fervent supporters.

The January 6 rally, which culminated in the attack on the Capitol, was seen as the direct result of this disinformation campaign. During his speech to the crowd before the assault, Trump used language that many interpreted as a call to violent action, urging attendees to "fight like hell" to take back their country. Trump's failure to respond forcefully during the hours of the assault—when he was asked to intervene and call on his followers to stand down—reinforced the narrative that he was willing to let violence undermine the democratic process.

Additionally, theories emerged that certain members of Trump's inner circle, including some Republican lawmakers, had prior knowledge of the plans to storm the Capitol or, at the very least, did not do enough to stop the violence. This led to speculation about the existence of a broader conspiracy aimed at preventing the certification of the electoral results and keeping Trump in power illegitimately. Although these theories have not been confirmed, and legal efforts to hold Trump accountable proved insufficient for a conviction, the attack left an indelible mark on the fragility of American democracy.

Trump's second impeachment. Donald Trump's role in inciting the assault became the subject of widespread debate. Many of his critics pointed to his speech beforehand as a direct trigger for the violent events. In response, the House of Representatives passed Trump's second impeachment on January 13, 2021, accusing him of "incitement of insurrection." This made him the first president in U.S. history to face impeachment twice.

Although the Senate did not convict Trump, the trial left an indelible stain on his legacy. Nationally, the country was engulfed in debates about the responsibility of public figures and the dangers of incendiary rhetoric.

Impact on American politics. The attack on the Capitol represented not only a physical assault on the building but also an existential crisis for American democracy. The events of January 6 further exacerbated the deep political polarization already present in the country. The violence perpetrated by Trump supporters served as a warning about the power of conspiracy theories and extremism, which had been growing under the influence of social media and incendiary political rhetoric.

In the aftermath of the attack, unprecedented security measures were introduced in Washington, D.C., including a strong military presence for Joe Biden's inauguration on January 20, 2021. Additionally, changes were made to security procedures within the Capitol to prevent future attacks, as well as a series of congressional investigations to understand the failures that led to the security collapse that day.

Lessons for democracy. The assault on the Capitol is a grim reminder of how democracies, even those with strong institutions, are vulnerable when leaders undermine trust in electoral processes and when public discourse transforms into incitement to violence. The lessons of January 6, 2021, continue to resonate in American politics, with long-term implications for how to address disinformation, national security, and extremism.

Here is the translation of the chapter from Spanish to English, maintaining the Anglo-Saxon narrative style:

Chapter 11: The Assassination Attempt on Donald Trump and Its Repercussions on the 2024 Campaign

As the 2024 presidential race began to gain traction, an unexpected event shook the country: an assassination attempt against Donald Trump, the former president seeking his return to the White House. This event not only shocked his base of supporters but also had significant implications for the political landscape of that contest.

The Assassination Attempt

The attack on Trump occurred at a critical moment in his campaign. While heading to one of his rallies in a key state, security forces intercepted a plan orchestrated to end his life. The attempt was thwarted, but news of the plot spread quickly nationally and internationally, generating an immediate debate about the safety of public figures in the United States.

Although Trump emerged unharmed, the incident revealed the growing political tensions and the dangers associated with the country's increasing polarization. The attack also fueled the narrative of some sectors that promoted conspiracy theories surrounding his figure, arguing that he was the target of a "system" that sought to eliminate him.

Reactions and Political Repercussions

Immediately after the assassination attempt, reactions from the political class and the public were swift. Leaders from both Democratic and Republican parties strongly condemned the attack. Joe Biden, the incumbent president, offered a public statement emphasizing the importance of respecting political differences without resorting to violence.

For Trump, however, the attack became a centerpiece of his campaign rhetoric. In his subsequent public appearances, he emphasized that the attempt on his life was proof of the powerful enemies he faced and the fight he was waging on behalf of "the forgotten" in America. The narrative that he was a victim of a political plot was reinforced by his most loyal followers, and the attack only increased the loyalty of his electoral base.

Impact on the 2024 Campaign

At a strategic level, the assassination attempt altered the course of the presidential campaign. Security became a crucial issue in the debates, and candidates found themselves forced to speak not only about their political vision but also about the growing wave of political violence in the country. Trump capitalized on the incident, presenting himself as the only candidate willing to fight against the "corrupt system" that, according to him, was willing to do anything to prevent his return to power.

This event also increased the level of protection around political figures and generated new conversations about the need to reform security and protection laws for presidential candidates.

Long-term Repercussions

The attack not only had immediate repercussions on the campaign but also left a mark on the political discourse of the United States. The narrative of Trump as a "victim" of a corrupt system resonated among his followers, who redoubled their support at subsequent rallies. However, for his opponents, the attack was a reflection of the danger of the incendiary rhetoric that had characterized his campaign.

In the long term, the assassination attempt raised questions about the stability of American politics and the limits of polarization. As the 2024 elections approached, the event served as a somber reminder of the inherent risks in a deeply divided democracy.

Chapter 12: Future Prospects and Lasting Legacy

Donald Trump's presidency was a unique period in the political history of the United States. From his surprising election in 2016 to his controversial exit in 2021, Trump left an indelible mark on American politics and the world's perception of the country.

In this chapter, we will explore the future prospects and lasting legacy of Donald Trump. This will include an analysis of how his presidency impacted both the domestic and foreign policy of the United States, as well as its effect on party politics and the electoral system. We will also consider how his leadership style and communication approach might influence future politics and leadership.

Additionally, we will address questions about how Trump will be remembered in history, the divisions his presidency left in American society, and his impact on the image and role of the United States on the global stage.

Donald Trump's presidency sparked passionate reactions and divergent opinions, and his legacy remains a topic of debate and analysis. This chapter aims to offer a balanced perspective and insight into the potential future trajectories of his legacy, with the goal of better understanding his lasting impact on American politics, society, and the world.

Donald Trump's Role in Post-Presidential Politics

Donald Trump's role in post-presidential politics has been one of the most prominent and debated issues since his departure from the White House.

Donald Trump continues to be an influential figure in American politics, even after leaving the presidency in 2021. His influence can be seen in several areas, including:

- **The Republican Party**: Trump remains a very popular figure within the Republican Party. His support is essential for Republican candidates, and his influence has helped radicalize the party.
- **American Politics**: Trump remains a highly visible figure in American politics. His comments and actions continue to make news, and his influence has helped polarize the country.
- **Global Politics**: Trump has also had an impact on global politics. His authoritarian leadership style has inspired other populist leaders, and his influence has contributed to the fragmentation of the world order.

It is likely that Trump will remain an influential figure in American politics for many years. His influence is complex and multifaceted, but it is undeniable that he has had a significant impact on the country.

Some possible scenarios for Trump's role in post-presidential politics include:

- **A Return to the Presidency**: Trump has made it clear that he wants to return to the presidency in 2024. If he wins the Republican nomination, he would be a highly competitive candidate.
- **A Leadership Role in the Republican Party**: Even if Trump does not return to the presidency, he could continue to play a leadership role in the Republican Party. His support could be

essential for Republican candidates, and his influence would help keep the party united.
- **A Role as a Political Commentator**: Trump could continue to be a public figure, commenting on American politics. His influence would help keep political issues in the spotlight and continue to polarize the country.

It is impossible to say for certain what Trump's role in post-presidential politics will be. However, it is likely that he will remain an influential figure in the country for many years.

Below are some key aspects of his role in post-presidential politics:

1. **Activism and Leadership in the Republican Party**:
    - Trump has maintained an active profile in the Republican Party and has influenced the direction of the party. His leadership and ability to mobilize a base of followers have given him a prominent role in Republican politics.
    - He has endorsed Republican candidates in local elections and primaries and has intervened in elections to try to influence the selection of loyal candidates.
2. **Creation of the "Save America" PAC**:
    - After leaving the presidency, Trump founded the Political Action Committee (PAC) "Save America," which has raised funds and supported Republican candidates on a national level.
    - This PAC has been used to fund political campaigns, solidifying his influence within the party.
3. **Impact on the Political Agenda**:
    - Although no longer president, Trump has continued to shape the political agenda of the Republican Party.

Issues such as immigration, trade, and foreign policy have been influenced by his positions.
4. **Future Presidential Candidacies**:
    - There has been speculation about whether Trump will run for president again in the 2024 election. If he decides to run, his candidacy could significantly impact the Republican primaries and national politics.
5. **Legal Challenges and Judicial Problems**:
    - Trump also faces a series of legal challenges and judicial issues, including ongoing investigations into his finances, businesses, the Capitol riot, and the votes in Fulton.
6. **Continued Use of Social Media**:
    - Although he was temporarily suspended from several social media platforms after leaving the presidency, Trump has sought ways to stay in touch with his followers and communicate his political messages, often through statements and interviews in conservative media.

Trump's role in post-presidential politics is complex and constantly evolving. His influence in the Republican Party and American politics in general remains significant, and his presence will continue to be an important topic in political debates and the future direction of the United States.

His Influence on the Republican Party

Donald Trump's influence on the Republican Party has been a prominent factor in American politics since his presidency and has continued to be a powerful force in post-presidential politics. Here is an analysis of his influence on the Republican Party:

1. **Control of the Electoral Base**:

- One of the most notable aspects of Trump's influence on the Republican Party is his ability to mobilize and maintain a solid and loyal electoral base. Through his charismatic style and populist rhetoric, Trump has built a strong connection with a significant portion of Republican voters.

2. **Leadership of the Party**:
    - Trump remains a leading figure within the Republican Party, and many party leaders seek his endorsement and support in elections. His backing of Republican candidates can be decisive in primaries and general elections.

3. **Decision-Making in the Party**:
    - Trump has influenced the Republican Party's political agenda and policies. His focus on issues such as immigration, trade, and foreign policy has left a mark on the party platform.

4. **Partisan Polarization**:
    - Trump's influence on the Republican Party has also translated into increased polarization within the party and in American politics in general. His confrontational style and rhetoric have contributed to divisions between party factions.

5. **Challenges to Critical Members**:
    - Trump has publicly confronted Republican members who have been critical of him or who voted against him in the impeachment process. This has led to internal divisions and public disputes within the party.

6. **2024 Elections**:
    - Trump's influence will be a key factor in the 2024 presidential elections. His endorsement of

candidates and his decision to run or not will have a significant impact on the party's future direction.
7. **Challenges to the Party's Tradition:**
    - Trump's influence has also challenged some of the Republican Party's historical traditions and values, including its stance on issues such as international trade and foreign policy.
8. **The Rise of Far-Right Populism:**
    - Trump is a far-right populist, and his presidency helped popularize this ideology among Republicans.
9. **Shifts in the Party Agenda:**
    - Trump shifted the Republican Party's agenda further to the right, focusing on issues such as immigration, nationalism, and protectionism.

Trump's influence on the Republican Party is likely to continue in the coming years. If Trump decides to run for president in 2024, his influence will be even stronger.

However, it is also possible that Trump's influence will diminish over time. If Trump does not run for president in 2024, and if the Republican Party chooses a different leader, Trump's influence could begin to wane.

It is difficult to predict how Trump's influence on the Republican Party will evolve in the future. However, he is likely to remain an important influence in the party for many years.

Reflections on His Long-Term Impact on American Politics

In the long term, Trump's impact on American politics is yet to be fully realized. However, his presidency is likely to have a significant impact on the country for many years.

1. **Partisan Division and Polarization:**
    - Trump's presidency intensified partisan division and polarization in the United States. His

confrontational style and communication approach often exacerbated political differences. Polarization remains a significant challenge in American politics.

2. **Changes in the Political Agenda:**
    ◦ Trump influenced the U.S. political agenda by prioritizing issues such as immigration, trade, and deregulation. His emphasis on these issues has led to a rethinking of policies in these areas by both parties.

3. **Transformation of the Republican Party:**
    ◦ Trump left a deep mark on the Republican Party, redefining its positions on key issues. His influence has led to a reshaping of the party's platform and greater loyalty to his leadership.

4. **Effect on Relations with the World:**
    ◦ Trump's presidency also impacted international relations and the global perception of the United States. His focus on nationalism and often controversial rhetoric influenced how the world views America.

5. **Institutional Challenges and Political Norms:**
    ◦ Trump's presidency posed challenges to established political institutions and norms. His relationship with Congress, his use of executive orders, and his focus on disinformation raised concerns about the health of American democracy.

6. **Long-Term Legacy:**
    ◦ Trump's long-term legacy in American politics will depend largely on how future political events unfold. His ability to maintain a loyal base of followers and his influence within the Republican Party will remain key factors in his legacy.

Ultimately, Donald Trump's long-term impact on American politics is a developing issue that will be evaluated by future generations. His presidency left a significant imprint on U.S. politics, society, and culture, and it will continue to be the subject of analysis and reflection for decades to come.

Epilogue: The Future of American Politics

The future of American politics is filled with uncertainty and could take various directions depending on a number of factors. Here are some possible future scenarios and the consequences that could arise from them:

1. **Continuation of Polarization**:
    - **Scenario**: Political polarization in the United States could persist or even intensify in the coming years. The parties may continue to drift apart in terms of ideology and values.
    - **Consequences**: This could make it more difficult for Congress to reach agreements and pass significant legislation. Polarization could also lead to greater division in society and undermine trust in democratic institutions.
2. **Demographic and Generational Change**:
    - **Scenario**: Demographic changes and generational dynamics could influence U.S. politics as more diverse and younger groups gain political influence.
    - **Consequences**: This could lead to shifts in the political agenda, with a greater focus on issues such as climate change, racial equality, and healthcare. Political parties may need to adapt to attract these

groups.
3. **Electoral Reforms:**
    - **Scenario**: Significant reforms to the U.S. electoral system could occur, such as changes to the Electoral College or the implementation of nationwide mail-in voting.
    - **Consequences**: These reforms could alter the way elections are conducted and change the balance of power between states. They could also influence the electoral strategies of the parties.
4. **Return to Bipartisan Consensus:**
    - **Scenario**: There is the possibility that the U.S. could experience a return to bipartisan consensus, where leaders from both parties work together to address pressing issues.
    - **Consequences**: This could lead to the passage of significant legislation in areas such as infrastructure, healthcare, and immigration reform. However, it could also generate resistance among those who prefer a more polarized political landscape.
5. **Changes in Foreign Policy:**
    - **Scenario**: U.S. foreign policy could experience significant shifts depending on relations with other nations and global challenges such as climate change and international security.
    - **Consequences**: Changes in foreign policy could affect the U.S.'s position in the world and its relationships with allies and adversaries. New alliances and conflicts could emerge.
6. **Greater Civic Participation:**
    - **Scenario**: American citizens may become more

actively involved in politics, voting in local and national elections and engaging in civic activities.
- **Consequences**: Increased civic participation could strengthen American democracy and give a broader range of political perspectives a voice. It could also lead to greater scrutiny of political leaders.

It is important to remember that politics is dynamic and can evolve in response to a variety of factors. Future scenarios and their consequences will largely depend on the decisions made by citizens, political leaders, and changing circumstances. The future of American politics lies in the hands of those who participate in the political process and seek to shape the direction of the country.

Sources consulted

Https://www.jovenesenlaciencia.ugto.mx/index.php/jovenesenlaciencia/article/view/2093

https://www.bbc.com/mundo/noticias/2016/04/160413_economia_origen_fortuna_trump_lf

https://www.elfinanciero.com.mx/opinion/leonardo-kourchenko-el-globo/2023/08/29/los-juicios-de-trump/

https://www.biografiasyvidas.com/biografia/t/trump.htm

https://elpais.com/especiales/2015/donald-trump/

https://www.elfinanciero.com.mx/opinion/gustavo-de-hoyos-walther/2023/08/17/los-problemas-de-mr-trump/

https://es.wikipedia.org/wiki/Elecciones_presidenciales_de_Estados_Unidos_de_2020

https://verne.elpais.com/verne/2021/01/09/mexico/1610159462_800567.html

https://elpais.com/especiales/2020/elecciones-estados-unidos/resultados/

https://cnnespanol.cnn.com/video/cnnee-dusa-nyt-access-hollywood-trump-duda-video-veracidad-grab-them-by-the-pussy-acoso-sexual/

https://www.theatlantic.com/ideas/archive/2023/08/donald-trump-indictment-gop-jan-6/674895/

https://www.washingtonpost.com/politics/2023/03/29/polarization-trump-one-simple-poll-result/

https://elpais.com/especiales/2016/elecciones-eeuu/la-america-de-donald-trump/

https://elpais.com/internacional/2023-06-09/trump-admitio-en-una-grabacion-de-2021-que-tenia-documentos-confidenciales-mira-es-informacion-secreta.html

https://edition.cnn.com/politics

https://www.factcheck.org/2023/08/number-of-counties-won-in-presidential-election-doesnt-determine-outcome/

https://www.nytimes.com/spotlight/donald-trump

https://www.factcheck.org/2021/01/trumps-falsehood-filled-save-america-rally/

https://www.factcheck.org/2023/08/qa-on-trumps-georgia-indictment/

Milton Keynes UK
Ingram Content Group UK Ltd.
UKHW042002281024
450365UK00003B/92